Peter Downey is an author because he couldn't cut it as a musician. He lives in the suburbs with his wife, three children and four guinea pigs and drives a Tarago. He wrote this book because he believed somebody should warn dads-to-be about the enormous changes fatherhood will bring to their lives. He believes this to be more so than ever. He also wrote this book because he believes that our society needs more good dads. However, he primarily wrote this book so he could be a television and radio talk show celebrity and retire early to a villa in Portugal.

# PETER DOWNEY

# SO YOU'RE GOING TO BE A DAD

649
-1

NEW
ADDITION!

SIMON & SCHUSTER
AUSTRALIA

SO YOU'RE GOING TO BE A DAD

First published in Australia in 1994 by
Simon & Schuster (Australia) Pty Limited
Suite 2, Lower Ground Floor
14–16 Suakin Street
Pymble NSW 2073

A CBS Company
Sydney  New York  London  Toronto

This edition published 2005

Visit our website at www.simonsaysaustralia.com

Text © Peter Downey, 1994, 2005
Illustrations © Nik Scott, 1994

Quotes from *Parenthood* on pages vii, 30 and 191 copyright ©
by Universal City Studios, Inc. Courtesy of MCA Publishing Rights,
a Division of MCA Inc.

The National Library of Australia
Cataloguing-in-Publication data

Downey, Peter (Peter Douglas).
  So you're going to be a dad.

  New ed.
  Includes index.
  ISBN 978 0 7318 1268 4.

  1. Fatherhood.  2. Father and child.  I. Title.

306.8742

Cover and internal design by Lore Foye
Cover illustration by Lloyd Foye
Printed in Australia by Griffin Press
Typeset in 12/16pt Sabon by Kirby Jones

10 9 8 7 6 5 4

*This book is dedicated to my wonderful children,*
*whom I ignored for six months while I wrote a book*
*on how to be a good father.*

# AUTHOR'S NOTE

*You know ... when I was nineteen, Grandpa took me on the roller-coaster ... up ... down ... up ... down ... Oh, what a ride! Some didn't like it. They went on the merry-go-round. That just goes around ... nothing. I like the roller-coaster. You get more out of it.*

HELEN SHAW (GRANDMA), *Parenthood*

It is impossible in a book like this not to speak in generalisations. Every pregnancy is different. No labour experience is the same. Each baby is unique. Doctors' views differ. People have different attitudes and opinions. Practices change over time. Hospital policies vary. Averages, are just that – averages.

This book is obviously based on my own experiences, knowledge and opinions. Not everyone agrees with some of my ideas, but that's what's great about living in a democracy. All you have to do is look at the fiery parenting websites and bulletin boards out there to realise that some people are very passionate (read: 'psychopathic and obsessive') about matters pertaining to parenting. People go into battle over issues like circumcision, immunisation, breast-versus-bottle-feeding and even cloth versus disposable nappies, and if you don't agree with them then you must be some kind of DEMON FROM HELL and your child is destined for ruination. It is important that you don't simply adopt others' ideas on face value, but look into things more carefully and make up your own mind.

This is a general book, reflecting what I experienced and what I figure to be your run-of-the-mill suburban pregnancy, childbirth and parenting situation. I have erred on the side of simplicity and brevity and have avoided matters that require either great sensitivity or lengthy academic consideration. You will not find in this book any particular explorations of, for example, areas such as miscarriage, lotus births, umbilical cord storage, the particular issues posed by twins and triplets, attachment parenting or alternative medicines.

Some of the items I have covered here in a casual aside are the topics of 300-page books. So whatever you do, don't memorise this book as though it is a detailed, Sinai-delivered blueprint customised for your particular situation. You can't use this book for join-the-dot fathering. I have written it merely to give you a little information, raise some issues for you to discuss with your wife, and stimulate thought regarding what it means to be a dad.

In talking about the female person who will form the other half of the parenting team in your family, I have used the word 'wife' instead of 'partner'. Yeah, yeah, I know that, statistically speaking, probably half the guys who read this book will be unmarried and as such technically not a 'husband', but I had to choose one of them and I like the sound of 'wife' rather than 'partner'. Call me old-fashioned. But anyway, it's my book so I can do anything I damn well like.

In referring to the baby in the book, I have called it either 'the baby' or 'it'. I know *it* sounds impersonal and dehumanising, but I just couldn't make up my mind. So there.

## NOTES ON THIS REVISED EDITION

One night many years ago, when Meredith was pregnant with our first child, I sat at a computer and started typing out my thoughts and feelings about becoming a dad. It was a way of coping, I suppose, and seemed a better use of my time than sitting in a dark corner biting my fingernails. It began as a kind of diary, written to no one in particular, documenting my fears and experiences and discoveries as we navigated the unknown turf of pregnancy, childbirth and eventually parenthood.

Pretty soon the little journal had grown into a stack of pages full of anecdotes, facts, reflections and information. Several of my friends – fellow dads-to-be – started borrowing what I jokingly referred to as 'my book', and asking for more. And so it was that almost on a whim, I printed a copy and posted it off to Simon & Schuster to see if it was the kind of thing that would make a good book.

Without wanting to sound too grandiose … the rest, as they say, is history.

When I first wrote the Prologue to this book, I said that I wanted to become a rich and famous author and have a sticker on the front of the book declaring *Three Million Now in Print*. I had dreams of doing the talk-show circuit, driving an Audi TT Roadster, jetsetting around the international author scene and retiring to a villa in Portugal.

Well, I'm not quite there *yet*. I am neither rich nor famous. I haven't quite sold three million. I still drive a Tarago and am yet to put a deposit on that villa on the Atlantic coast.

Having said that – *here comes the wanker part of this spiel* – this book has done rather well. I did get to fly around and do a lot of talk-back radio and television and even enjoyed a couple of regular guest spots as a (wait for it) 'parenting expert'. The ABC filmed a documentary about me and my family. I have written, and continue to write, for a number of baby, parenting and men's magazines and I have even written a few other books. The first print run was reprinted, and then reprinted again and again. It is somewhere up near its seventeenth reprint, and it is now Australia's biggest selling and most popular book for new dads. It is selling in New Zealand, Canada and the UK. It has been translated into Turkish and an American version ('diapers' instead of 'nappies'!) is now published in the USA.

The best part, however, is the number of emails I get from guys (and funnily enough from their wives) from all over the world who have enjoyed reading the book. They are men of all ages and backgrounds who found the book a refreshing and honest portrayal of what they are themselves going through. They are thrilled to find that they are not alone in their feelings and on top of that, are pleased to find a more light-hearted fatherhood book which lacks the saccharine drippyness common to the genre. I take it as a great compliment that so many blokes have bothered to contact me to thank me for my musings.

*So You're Going To Be a Dad* first hit the shelves eleven years ago. And over that time, a lot of things have changed. Hence the need for this second, newly updated and freshly revised edition. The large bulk of the text is the same (if it ain't busted, don't try to fix it), but there a lot of practices and theories – from the trivial to the significant – relating to pregnancy, childbirth and parenting that are very different now to when I was first elbow-deep in a nappy. For example, some changes have been legal (attitudes to videotaping a caesarean birth in this increasingly litigious world); some changes have been technological (3D/4D ultrasounds and the incredible growth of parenting websites, bulletin boards and chat-rooms); some changes have come about due to the development of new products (jogger prams and the 'snappy'); some as the result of updated medical advice (SIDS prevention techniques); some changes are just a matter of shifts in the general body of parental practice (the availability of unisex 'parent change rooms' in airports and shopping centres, and changed attitudes towards circumcision, caesarean birth and weaning); and some changes I made are a simple reflection of my own lack of knowledge when I was initially writing the book (I had never even heard the words blastocyst, nausea gravidarum, meconium and colostrum before).

A lot has changed over that time in my own life, too. The words in this book paint a picture of a world far remote from the one in which I now live. Rachael, Georgia and Matilda are now in high school. Meredith went back to work. I am eleven years older and the clothes I had back then no longer fit me. So reading the book for me is like leafing through an old photo album full of pictures I can barely remember ... so much so that it's almost like reading about the experiences of someone else. Oh well, that's what happens I suppose. Time flies and kids grow up.

As I have read through this book, I sometimes feel that I come over as being too casual, too negative, too scared, too incompetent, too stupid and too ignorant. *Was I really like that?* Well ... yeah, I suspect I was. In revising this book, the temptation has been to change that tone, to reinvent and rewrite myself as a new dad who was confident, learned, positive, loving, capable and basically less of a whinger and a whiner than the bozo you read about here. As the dad of three young adolescent girls eleven years on, I feel like I want to grab my new-dad self by the collar, give me a good shake and say, 'Get over it and get on with it. It's not *that* hard. It's not *that* much of a big deal.' But that wouldn't be right. I don't want to discount those very real feelings and experiences I had just because I can't remember them now. It's too easy to reinterpret the past with the gift of retrospection and experience. So I have left my neurotic and inept self untouched. I hope you can relate to him ... I mean ... um, me.

I will say this, however, by way of closing. From shaky and hesitant beginnings, being a dad has been the best and most important and most enjoyable thing I have ever done in my life. It has redefined everything in my world from my daily timetable to my sense of self (and certainly my bank account!). Maybe that sounds scary from where you are right now, sitting reading this book and staring down the dark tunnel of impending fatherhood. But trust me ... on the other side of the tunnel the sun is shining, the grass is green and the water is fine.

I love being a dad. Every day is a new adventure. In fact, I wouldn't swap my spot in life with anyone ... not even Paul McCartney.

# CONTENTS

Author's note vii

Acknowledgments xv

Prologue 1

Chapter One: And so, it begins 7

Chapter Two: Pregnancy 32

Chapter Three: Time to get ready 58

Chapter Four: Surviving the hospital 106

Chapter Five: Surviving at home 140

Epilogue 193

Glossary 196

Appendix 1: Parent education films 205

Appendix 2: What my mates had to say 210

Index 220

# ACKNOWLEDGMENTS

Thanks to:

Meredith, my companion and wife, for her love, patience and total devotion to me and our children. It's easy to be a good dad when you've got a good mum by your side. I hope she remains as loving, patient and totally devoted when she discovers that I've published lots of personal stuff about her.

Rachael, Georgia and Matilda, my adorable girls. I couldn't have been a dad without you.

Hilda and Stan, my parents and role models, for always letting me know I was important.

Ray Farley, fellow author and father, for his coaching and rope-showing.

Sue Williamson, cousin and lactation consultant, who taught me all I know about breastmilk and scones.

Dr Stewart Montano, mate since primary school, for setting me straight about medical stuff and letting me join his Inventors' Club when we were in third class.

Dr Keith Hartman, obstetrician and Alfa driver, for his impressive professional skill and personal touch.

Pascale Beard for suggesting that *So You're Going To Be A Dad* is a catchier title than *Becoming A Dad: The Australian Bloke's Guide to Fatherhood*.

My original publishing team: Susan Morris-Yates, Executive Editor, for taking a chance with a new boy; Stephanie Pfennigwerth, my trusty editor, for the spit and polish in turning my scrawl into a fluent read; and Simon Schuster, Publisher and all-round great guy, for letting me use his chalet at Perisher. And ten years on, thanks to: Julia Collingwood, Managing Editor, and Jacquie Brown, Senior Editor, for championing this book for the next generation; eagled-eyed editor el-supremo Susan Gray whose attention to detail helped drag me kicking and screaming into the twenty-first century; and boss-man Jon Attenborough, who is just a swell guy.

And all my paternal comrades for their advice, anecdotes and fellowship as we walk the road together.

# PROLOGUE

Being a dad has its advantages and disadvantages. The advantages are:

- you can go to kids' films for half-price;
- you can hang out in toy shops without embarrassment;
- kind people let you into the front of queues;
- you can drive a people mover which looks like the 'Lost in Space' buggy; and
- you can break wind in a crowded room, and blame it on the baby.

The disadvantages are:

- it wrecks your life.

This is a book about being a dad. I've written it for three reasons.

Firstly, I want to become a rich and famous author. I hope this book ends up with one of those *Three Million Now in Print* stickers on it. This will mean that I can do the talk-show circuit, dress in black and consume macchiatos in inner-city cafés and then drive home in my Audi TT Roadster. I will jetset around the international author scene and retire to a villa in Portugal.

Secondly, I'm writing this book to warn you. Becoming a dad is life-changing. Somebody needs to prepare you. It might as well be me.

My wife Meredith and I are the proud parents of three daughters: Rachael, Georgia and Matilda. And I do mean proud. I love my kids. I love being their dad.

I loved it that time Rachael brought home some clay from preschool and thought she'd help me cook the evening meal by throwing a few chunks into my simmering pot of Chicken Marengo but I didn't realise until my guests started eating.

I loved it that time I left Georgia unsupervised for ten seconds and she knocked the receiver off the phone while simultaneously pressing the pre-set auto-dial of friends in New York which then connected with their answering machine but I didn't realise for well over an hour.

And I loved it that time I was dressed in a formal suit because I was going to a wedding in ten minutes and I went in for a final check on the kids and I picked up Matilda and the chunky stuff from her nappy oozed out onto my suit but I didn't have another one so I just had to wipe it down but all night during the reception people kept asking me, 'What's that curious aftershave you're wearing?'

Yep, there's nothing quite like being a dad. I consider myself a fully-fledged family man. Being a dad is really important to me. I wouldn't swap my spot in life with anyone, except maybe Paul McCartney. But I haven't always felt so strongly, and I certainly wouldn't say I have enjoyed every minute of it. As a new dad, I remember crawling into bed each night mumbling inanely to myself, *Why didn't anybody tell me about this? Why wasn't I warned? Can I change my mind about this whole dad thing?*

I remember feeling angry that I had been sold an ideal that being a dad was easy and fun and full of warmth and wonder and soft-focus moments all the time. I felt vaguely miffed that the male species had failed to adequately and truthfully prepare me for my new station in life. But then again ... I should have expected it. It was the same male species that brought me up believing that bucks' nights were loads of fun, strip clubs were elegant and sophisticated, and that getting blind drunk was a great way to spend an evening.

Becoming a father is a shock to the system. It's not like getting a new car or a new dog. So I'm writing to give you the lowdown, the scoop, the big picture, the man-in-the-street view.

Thirdly, I have a strong conviction about the importance of dadhood as an institution. Our country needs good dads. Our kids need good dads. What more noble cause can a man be involved in than playing a primary role in getting a member of the next generation ready to play their part in the world? And for too long have we dads taken a back seat in the parenting game!

It makes me happy that many modern men are pretty good at taking an active and involved role in their family life. Unfortunately, there is still an abundance of males in our society who view parenting as a maternal thing. They see their role as bread-winner and beer-drinker. This is a tragedy. As far as I can make out, the only parenting things that men can't do are:

- get pregnant in the first place;
- carry the baby for nine months;
- give birth;
- breastfeed; and
- remember the names of all the kids at playgroup.

Unfortunately, I have met dads who are not into family stuff, dads who seem permanently away on business, dads who are perpetually busy and are so wrapped up in their own lives that they and their children only ever pass like ships in the night. They are men with no time for family.

I was leafing through a stack of old magazines the other day when I came across an article on the new breed of workaholics in Australia; men who seem to live for their work and have little or no time for their own kids. It's my belief that one day these men will wake up and look at their children – who don't know them – and realise too late that there is more to life than work.

So in writing this book, I hope that I help some blokes realise how important and how enjoyable it is to be called 'Dad'.

*But how exactly do you 'be a dad'?*

Good question, but I'm not going to give away the secret here in the Prologue, otherwise you might not read the rest of the book.

Unfortunately, we males can't go to night school to get a Certificate of Fathering and, as far as I know, universities don't offer Bachelor degrees in Paternity. And an apprenticeship with the guy down the road who has a three-month-old is probably out of the question.

So how do we, as aspiring fathers-to-be, learn the ropes of fathering without hanging ourselves, so to speak?

When my wife Meredith was pregnant with our first child, Rachael, I had a thousand questions which needed answering. There were plans to be made and things to do and I knew nothing about kids. And I do mean *nothing*. I needed information. I needed lots of information. And the best source of information, of course, was the blokes who had trail-blazed the fathering path ahead of me. I would corner some poor unsuspecting new father at work or at a dinner party and grill him about all the intricacies of pregnancy, labour, nappies, feeding and fatherhood.

I haunted shops looking for decent books that would prepare me for dadhood. Unfortunately, most seem to be written exclusively for women (I could tell because the covers sported soft-focus photos of models silhouetted against frosted windows, with cushions stuffed up their jumpers). I did find a few books written just for dads, but they were either so dry or thick that they scared me off, or else were written by 'parenting experts' with horn-rimmed glasses, woollen vests and chequered trousers.

That's when I decided to write this.

The question you may be asking at this moment is, who exactly is Peter Downey to be telling me about all this stuff anyway?

Yet another good question.

Well, I'm not a medical doctor or a researcher. I'm not a child psychologist. I'm not a learned obstetrician or paediatrician. My qualification is that I'm an ordinary bloke, probably just like you. I live in the suburbs, work five days a week, wash the car on the weekend and like to get a DVD and Thai takeaway on a Friday night.

Then one day I became a dad.

One day I was a normal, carefree guy, just like you. The next day I was buying nappies and learning how to assemble a travel cot.

So here I am, a few years down the track, ready to share my joys, frustrations, ideas and mistakes. If that doesn't convince you, though, I've watched plenty of films and TV shows with dads and babies in them.

My basic message in this book is that being a dad takes energy, commitment and involvement. It takes a lot of time and effort. You can't do it half-heartedly. You can't do it in your spare time. This is very important for you to understand, so I'm going to write it again.

Being a dad takes energy, commitment and involvement. It takes a lot of time and effort. You can't do it half-heartedly. You can't do it in your spare time.

It means being active and involved in the daily dealings with your baby. It means 'getting your hands dirty' and participating in all aspects of family life. It means sharing the parenting and rejecting stereotypes that dictate parenting is for women only. If you still haven't got the point yet, read this paragraph again.

And before I come under attack for the inherent sexism in the pages that follow, let me say that this book is for blokes. I wrote it with the Australian male in mind; the Australian male who knows little or nothing about fatherhood, but who is keen to have a good go at it.

But in concentrating almost exclusively on the dad, let me just say that by no means do I consider men to have a more important role than women in the rearing of children. Parenting is a team game. Mums are equally as important as dads. I have nothing against women. In fact, I like women.

I even married one.

So welcome to the wonderful world of fatherhood. We have a long road ahead of us. A hard road. A road fraught with obstacles, trials and tribulations. But it is also a rewarding road, peppered with great experiences and golden moments that you wouldn't have thought possible. And once you walk the road, you'll never be the same again.

So, good luck on your journey.

You'll need it.

# CHAPTER ONE

# AND SO, IT BEGINS

*'If only I could have seen the writing on the wall.*
*It would have said, "Your wife's pregnant! Run away!*
*Run away!"'*

## SEX AND ITS SIDE EFFECTS

*WARNING: The Surgeon General advises that sex may cause children.*

Sex is an appropriate starting point for us to commence our consideration of fatherhood. After all, this is where the journey begins.

By the very virtue of the fact that you are actually reading this page, I can safely assume that you have already passed this initial but very crucial test. With flying colours. For this reason, and in the interests of good taste, I shall refrain at this point from elaborating any further on how much fun you had in the process and 'was it good for you too, baby?', etc.

But we all get the message. While you were lying back in the haze of post-coital euphoria – like they do in the movies – an armada of about 300 million of your sperm set off from Port Penis on the first leg of their marathon six-inch (or so) swim through all that female plumbing, the names of which I can never quite remember.

(I will probably never come to terms with all those bits and pieces of the female anatomy. As an adolescent, sitting in a PD class at an all-boys' school, I was always perplexed by the textbook cross-sections of women's insides. You know the picture I mean? That's right, the diagram of the one-legged woman. I could never follow all the bulbous squiggles and channels with the funny names. In fact, it was only years later that I discovered that the cross-section diagram was in fact a *side* view, not a *top* view. Maybe I should have paid more attention, instead of sitting up the back of the classroom with Paul Brinkman trying to put diaphragms on our heads like swimming caps.)

Anyway, while nothing to you, those inches are like a veritable Sydney Harbour to these little tadpoles. They will only

*cross-section of women's insides ...*

survive for a few days, so there is no time to waste. Like salmon battling their way upstream, they have to swim from the vagina, north through the uterus (or womb), and climb up one of the two Fallopian tubes to where an egg is hiding. It's like an Olympic marathon, and there can only be one winner. There are no consolation prizes. If they don't win the victor's crown (the 'egg' or 'ovum'), they're out of the picture for good. And with odds like 300 million to one – much worse than any lottery game played in the history of humankind – the competition is fierce. Imagine it, basically, as a 100-kilometre swimming race against the entire population of India.

An hour or so later, with the swim mostly over (probably while you were snoring loudly and were totally oblivious to the creative energies you had unleashed upon the world), only a few thousand of the strongest sperm have survived the journey. The finalists have navigated the obstacles and the plumbing with the complicated names and have located the prize – the golden egg.

Now, this is not an egg in the chicken-type hard-boiled, fried or sunny-side-up sense of the word. It is more like a dot. A cell. A little pin-prick. A dot on the back of a cell sitting in the middle of a pinprick. The point is, it is very, very tiny. It makes the full-stop at the end of this sentence look like a beach ball.

Like the sperm, the egg too has undergone a journey of its own. Women have about half a million of these ova stored in their ovaries. Each month during ovulation, the mature or 'ripe' ovum leaves its sisters and bobs on down one of the Fallopian tubes, like a little planet waiting for the strange aliens with the tails to come and visit.

So it sits there, waiting.

Waiting.

Waiting.

Time is critical, because this ovum has a 'use-by' date of only about twenty-four hours. So for the next couple of hours after their journey, all the remaining spermatic contenders go into Stage Two of their biathlon, which is basically a head-butting competition. The sperms all find a spot on the ovum they can call their own, stick their heads down and start spinning around and around like fence-post diggers. Picture a basketball swarming with animated alfalfa sprouts. The winner is the one who breaks the ovum wall and gets in first.

Two things immediately happen. The tail breaks off from the head of the sperm and the ovum gets coy and undergoes a chemical change which instantly shuts out all the other contenders. It's a bit of a disappointment for them, I should imagine; getting all that way only to be pipped at the post just because they couldn't dig fast enough. But it's a jungle out there. I guess they probably get depressed and swim around until they die.

Sad, really.

Anyway, what you have then is a fertilised egg sitting in its own little dark, warm universe. You can almost imagine the Starship *Enterprise* zooming past through this microscopic universe with Spock at the viewscreen musing, *'It's life, Jim ... but not as we know it.'*

And there you have it. The egg is officially fertilised. The wheels of fate have spun in their diurnal course and although you don't know it yet, you're going to be a dad.

This is the miracle of life. The miracle of sex. And it *is* a miracle.

God really was very clever to have thought it up.

This child of yours is unique in the universe. You and your wife are the only combination in history who could have created it. Think of it this way: your wife has about half a million ova. You have about 300 million sperm per ejaculation. Let us assume, for the sake of argument, that you have sex once a week over a ten-year potential parenting period. Your child could be *any combination* of any single sperm and any single ovum. So if my mathematics serves me correctly (which it might not do, considering I got 42 per cent for my final exam), then that makes your child one of 78 000 000 000 000 000 (78 quadrillion) possible people combinations.

*God really was very clever to have thought it up ...*

This is a humbling thing for a father to contemplate. Without getting into a philosophical debate, it's kind of awesome to think about the infinitesimal beginnings of human life – the beginnings of the life of your child. What is at this point an indistinct speck will grow to be a person whom you will know and love intimately – a person, I might add, who will change your life and take you into a world you could not have possibly imagined.

You will see this infinitesimally small spot learn to crawl, walk and talk. It will create bizarre drawings for you to stick on your fridge and say great stuff like, 'Why aren't I a tree?' It will get dressed up as a bear for school play night. It will make you cold tea and burnt toast on Father's Day. You will worry when it goes out on its first date, and you will lie awake at night because it borrowed your car and is two hours late in getting home. This dot will take you to the peaks of pleasure ('I love you, Dad') and to the depths of despair ('Dad, I've got a mobile phone bill for over $1000'). And then one day that microscopic cell will leave home and you'll wonder what you ever did before it came along.

## MORNING SICKNESS

Of course, at this stage you are probably still unaware you are travelling down the road to dadhood. The thing is, you don't turn on the evening news and hear:

*'A bulletin just to hand ... your wife became pregnant yesterday in what is being referred to as a nocturnal orgy of sex. Early reports indicate that both mother and father are in a stable condition ...'*

Similarly, the stork doesn't wake you up in the morning by tapping on your bedroom window and squawking, 'YOUR WIFE'S PREGNANT! BRAAA! YOUR WIFE'S PREGNANT! BRAAA!'

But there *is* a telltale sign. An early warning system, if you like. Its medical name is the grandiosely titled 'nausea gravidarum', but most people just refer to it as *morning sickness*.

One day a few years ago (in our glory days, when we were DINKs), I accompanied Meredith to get a haircut. The salon was half-full of women getting perms and rinses and other things out of my experience and beyond my comprehension. Everything was going fine until my wife unexpectedly leapt up and staggered into the bathroom at the rear of the shop. For the next few minutes we all sat there perplexed by the cacophony of gurgling and gagging, beautifully amplified by the tiled walls and floor of the salon.

At the time, I simply assumed this sudden and violent illness was due to my substandard attempt at a chicken laksa the previous evening. I don't think I'd even heard of morning sickness before. But that sickness was the trumpet blast that heralded the end of one era of my life, and the approach of a new one: dadhood.

If only I could have seen the writing on the wall. It would have said, 'Your wife's pregnant! Run away! Run away!' But back then I was naive and ignorant about such things. You see, on the outside my wife looked fine and normal. From the TV I had learnt that pregnant women were supposedly huge and cumbersome, that they waddled when they walked, and that they dressed in tents. But my wife was slim and attractive, she sauntered when she walked and she was wearing jeans; *ergo*, she was not pregnant.

But on the *inside*, that sperm and ovum combination was hard at work on its human cocktail. And you can't have another person starting to grow within your own personal body space without certain effects on your own wellbeing. The presence of the fertilised egg causes the mother's body to secrete a nasty hormone called Beta hCG. Meredith's blood and major body systems had gone into overdrive. One small side effect was that she felt nauseous.

They call this 'morning sickness'. It's like being carsick, except that it keeps going even when you get out of the car. It's similar to the sensation you get when you scoff a seafood platter, a dozen raw eggs, a large chocolate sundae and a few schooners before going for a spin on a roller-coaster. It usually lasts for three months, but in some cases it can last the entire pregnancy. The term 'morning sickness' is something of a misnomer, because it can happen all day. To be accurate, it should be called 'morning, afternoon and night sickness', but this doesn't really roll off the tongue as well.

There is only one positive aspect to morning sickness. Some research has found that women who suffer from morning sickness have fewer miscarriages. So it may be a sign that a fertilised egg has implanted successfully. This quirky statistic, however, may be of little comfort to your wife as she throws up into a pot plant at your local shopping centre.

## CONFIRMING THE OBVIOUS

Some women know that they are pregnant within a few weeks of conception. Their biological systems start ringing alarm bells and they soon put two and two together. But you also hear stories about women who go to their doctor with a suspected gallstone problem only to find their gallstone has eyes, hands and a heartbeat and is already eight months old. Obviously, their biological alarm bells did not ring loud enough. They put two and two together but ended up with five.

However, quite a few mums I know assure me that most women know when they are pregnant. 'It's just one of those instinctive things,' they say. Being a guy, I'm not sure about the validity of this comment, but I guess there must come a point in every woman's pregnancy when she begins to suspect that something is going on down in the engine room. It might be because of a missed period. It might be because her breasts have become sore or because she is suddenly moody or tired. It might be because of an unexpected propensity to vomit, even when you didn't cook the night before. It may well even be 'just one of those instinctive things'.

Once the woman reaches this point, however, things really start to heat up. She can go to either the chemist or the doctor to have her suspicions confirmed with a pregnancy test. Home pregnancy tests are about 99 per cent accurate and are best done first thing in the morning.

Ah, the marvels of modern medical science! This test is really quite amazing and is certainly worth seeing. It measures the level of Beta hCG secreted into the mother's urine because of the suspected internal intruder. There are a couple of different tests available on the market but they all basically involve introducing urine to some type of test strip. Some tests are even done 'midstream', for those who like to live dangerously.

Meredith used a test that looked like a credit card. Four or five drops of urine were dripped onto one corner of the card. The urine then seeped across to the other corner, passing through a little viewing window *en route*. Five minutes later, she watched as a little cross appeared in the window, confirming her suspicions. We were going to be parents.

You can even keep this little card or test strip in your wallet. It's a great conversation starter at the pub or over the dinner table, that is if you can put up with the smell.

## AND NOW, THE NEWS

As far as I can make out, there are basically two types of fathers. Firstly, there are the fathers who *have been trying* to become fathers. 'We've been *trying* now for about six months,' he will pipe up cheerily over an after-work pint of ale. This word *trying* is a great euphemism. What it basically means is that he has been having sex a lot. He has talked it over with his wife and they have both been *trying* for a long time to get it all happening. For some, this is a very long, complicated and frustrating process, perhaps involving thermometers, calendars and visits to the doctor – maybe even a visit to that special doctor in the city who gives you a glass jar and says, '*Third cubicle on the right, if you would please, sir.*'

Anyway, the bottom line is that this type of father and his wife have been working hard at getting pregnant; at becoming parents, mother and father, mum and dad. He is expectant and is keenly waiting, planning and preparing for the missed period and those magically whispered words, '*Darling, I'm pregnant.*'

Then there is the second type of father. He is the one who has *not* been trying to become a father. (However, this doesn't necessarily mean that he hasn't been having sex a lot.) Perhaps in the heat of passion he and his wife brushed aside the security of contraception. Perhaps the contraception failed. Maybe they simply forgot that sex causes children. Perhaps they just wanted to see what would happen. Of course, he could just be plain stupid.

Anyway, the bottom line is that *this* type of father enjoyed sex largely for relational purposes, as opposed to specifically 'extending the family tree' purposes. He is *not* expectant and is *not* keenly waiting, planning and preparing for the missed period and those magically whispered words, '*Darling, I'm pregnant.*'

Now, both of these guys have two things in common:

- in just a few months, they will both become fathers; and
- there will come a day soon where this important fact is revealed to them.

At this specific point, they will probably have fairly distinct and different responses to the actual news that fatherhood is nigh. Let's examine the different scenarios:

**Father Type I** – the one who has been *trying* – may experience the standard middle-class television scenario. Coming home from a busy day at work, he will throw his stuff into a corner and yell out, 'Damn head office! That contract I've just spent months on won't be ready till November. As if I don't have enough work around Christmas as it is.'

To which his wife, coming down the stairs, will respond, 'Well, don't make too many plans for the end of the year.'

(At this point wafting violins will start to swell in the background. He will eye her hopefully.)

'You mean ... '

'Yes, darling, I saw Dr Lloyd this afternoon.'

(Crescendo of violins. Counter-melody subtly and harmoniously introduced by cellos and violas.)

'You mean ... '

'Yes, my love. The tests were positive.'

(Massive crescendo. Whole symphony joins in.)

'You mean ... '

'Yes, my honey blossom pancake ... you're going to be ... (and then the magical words as the whole room starts to spin uncontrollably, accompanied by beautiful orchestral themes) A DAD.'

He will experience a sensation of being lifted off the ground. He will soar above the trees and spin around amongst the clouds. Clutching his wife to him, he will feel deep inner warmth and fulfilment. It is a beautiful moment, full of symphonies and fireworks.

**Father Type II** – the one who has *not been trying* – may have something of a different experience. Coming home from a busy day at work, he will throw his stuff into a corner and yell out, 'Damn head office! That contract I've just spent months on won't be ready till November. As if I don't have enough work around Christmas as it is.'

To which his wife, coming down the stairs, will respond, 'Well, don't make too many plans for the end of the year.'

(At this point he will hear the theme from *Jaws* waft menacingly through the air. He will eye her suspiciously.)

'What are you talking about?'

'Darling, I saw Dr Lloyd this afternoon.'

(Crescendo of *Jaws* theme. Aggressive counter-melody suddenly introduced à la staccato stabs from *Psycho*.)

'Yeah, so?'

'I had some tests. They were positive.'

(Massive crescendo of timpani and other nastily percussive instruments.)

'You mean ...'

'I'm pregnant. You're going to be ... (and then the room will spin sickeningly to the deafening chorus of cannons, breaking glass and sirens) A DAD.'

He will experience the curious sensation of being clubbed across the forehead with a cricket bat while toppling backwards over a precipice and into a pit of molten lava and broken glass. His head will swim and his knees buckle. He will clutch his wife to him so he doesn't fall over. He may even experience inner warmth as his bladder malfunctions. His jaw will flop about and, in a feeble attempt at speech, he will produce only pathetic squeaks and gurgles.

In this situation, it is important for the moment to be handled delicately. For example, there are certain things that should not be said, such as:

- *How the hell did that happen?*
- *Have you seen the remote?*
- *I've got footy training.*
- *So?*
- *We can't afford it.*
- *What's for dinner?*
- *That's fine, but don't expect me to get involved.*

All of these comments are things that blokes might have said back in the good old days. But come on, this is the twenty-first century. We're all Sensitive New Age Guys.

Aren't we?

By the way, when your wife says she's pregnant, DON'T – whatever you do, DON'T – say, 'Oh, you better sit down.' They only say that on TV.

If you're a father type I, you probably feel pretty good. If you're a father type II, don't feel too bad. I've been a father type II three times now and it hasn't done me any harm. Not that my wife and I were irresponsible or stupid or anything like that. Meredith had been on the Pill for a while, and for various and personal reasons, which are frankly none of your business, we both decided that she should come off the Pill. Our basic idea was that nature would take its course and she would fall pregnant eventually and whenever that happened would be just fine.

It happened the next day.

Call me naive, but I thought that pregnancy was actually a pretty difficult thing to achieve and that our 'nature's course' method would take a while. According to research, even if the sperm and ovum timing is ideal and the conditions are right, there is still only a 30 per cent chance of fertilisation. We have since discovered, however, that we are as fertile as the Nile Delta and only need to drink from the same coffee cup for Meredith to start feeling sick in the morning.

I clearly remember the day I found out my life was about to take off in a new and radical direction. I was sitting at my desk waiting for Meredith to pick me up after work. It was the eighth of March.

She'd needed the car that day because she was going to the doctor. She hadn't been her usual self since that emergency at the hairdresser's. It was a bit of a concern, really.

She waltzed in, looking totally cool and normal, and said hi. We engaged briefly in some light chat and then headed out through the drizzle that had plagued Sydney for the past few months. My mind was filled with thoughts of what we were going to have for dinner. Pizza? No, a chicken dish ... or those Mexican things. What are they called?

'Peter, what are you doing on October the twenty-fourth?' asked she.

'Nothing,' I replied, eyeing her sideways. 'Why, what have you got in mind?'

Of course! *Tacos.*

'Parenthood,' said she, with a mischievous grin.

Or are they *nachos*?

Parenthood.

*Nachos.*

Parenthood.

No, not *nachos.* The soft wrap ones ... um ... yes, *burritos*!

Parenthood.

The word spun inside my head for a few seconds, trying desperately to find something to grasp onto, but all it found were mental cookbooks. Toasted sandwiches, perhaps?

'I beg your pardon?' This is what I meant to say, but my mouth mumbled something more along the lines of, 'E bed du plarnd?'

And there was that word again. 'Parenthood,' she said. 'I'm pregnant. We're going to be parents.'

There was a moment's silence. Somewhere, a cricket chirped.

'You're going to be a dad.'

She smiled. Cool. Collected.

I wobbled. Shocked. Flushed.

Time stood still. My mind scrambled.

A father.

The words slowly sank in.

A *father*? Aren't they the guys you see on the expressway during school holidays, perched behind the wheel of a Tarago filled to bursting with mattresses, bikes, and assorted domestic detritus and through the fingerprint-encrusted window you can see the slightly crazed look on their face ... the kind of look that only comes as one enters the eighth hour of listening to repetitive jangly songs about rabbits and choo choo trains?

A *FATHER?* Aren't they the bedraggled-looking blokes you see at the DVD store surrounded by a tribe of runny-nosed munchkins whining whining whining about wanting to watch *The Lion King* again?

A father? Me? My father is a father! *His* father was a father! I'm only a son. Worse, I'm just a boy, a child. I've only just left home. I can't even iron my shirts properly. Panic! Changing nappies? Me?

Mayday ... Mayday ... I'm going down!!!!!! What about sleep? What about our mortgage? What about that overseas trip we were planning?

And what about dinner?

At this moment, one of my students passed by. 'Hello sir, how are you going?' he piped up.

*If only you knew, mate*, I thought. *If only you knew.*

By the way, we had leftovers for dinner.

## HOW DO YA FEEL?

This was my introduction to the wonderful world of fatherhood. One minute I was coasting along through life at a happy pace. I was in control and was closely following 'the plan'. Our young married lives were progressing nicely and the bank balance told us we were gradually finding our feet. The next minute, my life was spinning madly out of control on some bizarre and most unexpected tangent. Our future was suddenly plunged into the abyss of new and unexplored terrain.

Some men are thrilled and excited to hear the news of their impending dadhood. Some feel delirious and 'over the moon'. I felt a whole lot of emotions at once.

The prime one was *guilt*. I felt guilty that I wasn't ecstatic. I felt guilty that I didn't rush forward and grab my wife and say, 'I love you', or something like that. It wasn't like in the movies at all. Why didn't I feel ... *paternal?* Where was the symphony orchestra? To be blunt, it took me a little while to warm to the idea.

In a way, I also felt *excited*. I didn't really know what lay ahead of me, but the news brought that kind of expectant, nervy thrill you get when something really big is about to happen. It was the same sensation I experienced as a child, queuing up for a ride at the Easter Show while listening to the screams of fear from those already inside.

I was struck dumb by the awesomeness of the moment and felt that some philosophical and momentous words were in order. In a kind of slow-motion haze, I put my hand on Meredith's stomach and mumbled something grandiose about how, just centimetres away, under the skin, a new life was forming.

'No,' she said, moving my hand, 'just centimetres away under the skin is my bladder. The baby is *here*.'

Another feeling I had was *fear*. I felt it in the pit of my stomach and tasted it in my mouth. I was scared of this great big thing called *fatherhood*, now rushing inevitably towards me like a freight train. I was scared of the unknown. I knew absolutely nothing about babies. And I do mean *absolutely nothing*. I never even liked holding other people's babies. Come to think of it, I still don't.

It wasn't that I was opposed to the idea of becoming a father. It just took me by surprise, that's all. I mean, I didn't even suspect that Meredith was pregnant. To my mind there was no subtle lead-up, no hints at what was to come. So I felt shocked and awkward that this was not another of our carefully laid, middle-class-young-upwardly-mobile-couple plans. I could not even begin to comprehend what the words 'you're going to be a dad' meant. I knew how to teach *Hamlet* and how to cook a reasonable Tom Kah Gai. But a baby? You must be kidding! It all seemed so big and scary.

So *life-changing*.

Since then, in chatting with lots of blokes all over the place, I have discovered that this is not such an uncommon experience. I've come to realise that it's all right to feel shock and guilt and the burden of responsibility. It's all right to feel inadequate and scared. Fatherhood *is* a big and scary prospect. It's not something that can be digested and dealt with in a few minutes, or learned by glancing through cute anecdotes from the *Reader's Digest* in your doctor's waiting room.

Don't be so self-indulgent that you forget that your wife is also having the baby. Oh yes ... you remember now. She may well be feeling the same way. On top of which, she has the added anxiety of disruption to her work and nine months of increasing bodily discomfort, only to be topped off by incredible physical pain during the birth, midnight breastfeeds and months of sheer exhaustion afterwards.

So talk it out with your wife. Discuss your fears, feelings and concerns. Share your expectations and ideas. Communicating and sorting out your feelings is a great way to establish the team philosophy of parenting, even at this early stage.

And remember, there's comfort in numbers. Bear in mind the fact that nearly every dad you know (including your own dad) probably felt just as out of their depth as you do. Not one single dad alive was born into the role; it is a role you grow into. Bit by bit. Day by day. And if the millions of other guys on the planet can do it, then odds are on that you can too.

Nobody expects you to be an instantaneous parent. You're not supposed to be an expert in the blink of an eye. Even if you are totally stupid and extremely ignorant and hopeless with kids, it doesn't matter. You'll learn.

I did.

You'll be surprised at how little time it takes you to get used to the idea of fatherhood. And once you've recovered from the shock, it's time to start taking action.

There's much to be done and only a few months to go.

## LET'S GO PUBLIC

So where does that leave you now? To summarise, you have:

- had child-producing sex;
- found out that your baby will enter the world in a few months; and
- recovered from the initial shock.

The next stage can be pleasant or frightening, depending on:

- how you handle it; and
- whether or not your wife's family and friends actually *like* you.

I'm talking about *breaking the news* to people.

Watching the various reactions of family and friends – screams, fainting, hysterical laughter, weeping, muscle failure, casual nonchalance, etc. – can be a source of great amusement and the topic of dinner-time storytelling for years to come. But before you go telling everyone, there are a few things you should keep in mind.

Firstly, don't go public too early in the piece. It is important that you and your wife have a bit of space to get used to the idea of becoming parents before you go telling everybody. Wait a couple of days. Wait a couple of weeks. There's no rush. Once the cat's out of the bag, people will look at you differently. Everybody will want to give you advice and talk about parenting ad nauseam and have you around for dinner and start knitting little jackets and so on. Your conversations will be dominated by annoying questions and lengthy anecdotes ranging from the horrific ('Did we tell you about Jan's emergency caesar?') through the disgusting ('Anyway, Scottie pulled his nappy off in the car and when we stopped two hours later, the entire back seat was smeared with ...') to the plain mind-numbing ('But listen, one of the best features of this pram is this little Velcro tab here. See this Velcro tab? Watch what happens when I pull it ...'). Your friends and relatives will cease to look at you as 'a couple'; you will become 'parents-to-be'.

So you and your wife should stew over it for a while to get a bit more comfortable with the whole idea. Treasure your last moments together as 'a couple'.

Secondly, news about impending parenthood spreads faster than the bubonic plague. Research indicates that from the time you break the news to the first person, it only takes approximately forty-five seconds for every single person you have ever met in your entire life to find out that you're going to be a dad. You pull into a service station and the guy at the pump next to you, whom you swear you've never met before, winks at you and says, 'Hey mate, I heard your wife's up the sprout. Congratulations!'

This is particularly the case if you have one of those friends who loves to act as the community noticeboard. You know the type I mean. As soon as they hear any news of a vaguely gossipy or topical nature (i.e. engagements, births, pregnancies, divorces, retrenchments, socially awkward medical test results, etc.), they see it as their destiny in life to spread the word to everybody in their address book. This person can type an SMS in the time it takes you to say, 'We're going to have a ...'.

Tell this person last.

If you want to tell people yourself instead of letting them hear it on the grapevine, you have to time the announcement with the precision of a military operation. Once you go public, you have to do it *quickly*. If you don't, the surprise will be spoilt and everyone will know.

Thirdly, there are familial and peer politics to consider. In some families there is a 'pecking order' and if you don't pay heed to it, you may end up paying the price for the rest of your life. You know what I'm talking about. If you tell your neighbour before you tell your mother-in-law, there will be hell to pay. Like an elephant, she will never forget. (Just let me make it clear at this point that in no way do I consider *my* mother-in-law to be in any way like an elephant.)

Anyway, one of the best things about good news is telling other people, so that's just what we did.

First, my parents. We sat them down on the couch. With the benefit of hindsight, I could have handled it better. Not knowing how to broach the subject subtly, I jabbed my finger at Meredith and with a guilty-schoolboy look on my face, blurted, 'She's pregnant!'

My mother's legs did a little involuntary dance and her frame shuddered slightly. My dad, repeating his performance from the day we announced our engagement, sat there flapping his jaw and wearing a glazed expression on his face. When he stirred himself into action, several moments later, he pulled Meredith onto his knee and mumbled, 'You better sit down.'

Then we told my ninety-year-old great-aunt. 'WE ARE HAVING A BABY!' I yelled into her hearing aid.

'No, no gravy for me, thank you,' she replied with a smile.

My mother-in-law was pretty cool about the whole thing. We told her in the hallway of her flat as she came home from work laden with groceries. I was hoping she'd drop them, but I was disappointed.

Then there were our friends. One leapt screaming across a table at us while her husband had a small seizure. Another group of friends immediately broke out the warm champagne. One friend suddenly developed lockjaw, because his mouth didn't function for several seconds, and another one went into shock, because all he could do was constantly repeat sounds like 'Wwwoaaaahhhh'. Some of my less intellectual male friends nudged me in the ribs and leered, as if to say, 'We know what you two have been up to!' *Yeah, good thinking, guys.*

## MYTH BUSTING

Before we go any further with our exploration of fatherhood, now seems like a good time to explode some myths. Many of the expectations that I had as a new father turned out to be pure fiction. As a consequence, paternal reality turned out to be a bit of a slap in the face. And why? Because for many of us, our main source of information about many facets of the universe is that hideous mind-sucking box in the corner of the loungeroom – the television.

Unfortunately, television has proven to be an unreliable teacher across a whole range of human endeavour. The main problem is that a lot of what you see on television regarding *life* only takes place in the magical fantasy kingdom of TV-land. If you believe that what you see on the screen is reality, you will end up in trouble.

For example, regarding sex. Turn on the TV at any time of the day or night and there it is. When I got married, I carried with me the adolescent expectation that when I got home after a hard day's work, my negligee-clad wife would greet me at the door with a glass of champagne in her hand and a rose clamped between her teeth. Each night would herald a candle-lit feast, followed by nocturnal pleasures on an epic scale.

It wasn't like this. The TV lied.

The same applies to violence. The TV says that a gang of muscular martial arts thugs can bash you in the face and ribs with big lumps of wood and you can get away with only a dishevelled fringe. The TV says that when you get shot, you can grimace and get up again with all guns blazing. And I must have seen a hundred bottles smashed over a hundred heads in TV dramas. In real life, it's not the bottle that smashes.

Television also paints a different picture to reality with pregnancy, birth and, of course, fatherhood. Real-life pregnant women don't always stagger around groaning with their hands on their hips, and they don't need to sink awkwardly into a chair after every few steps they take. While food cravings are a normal part of pregnancy, it is generally not the dramatic middle-of-the-night crisis where you get woken and sent on an errand to the local service station to satisfy your wife's craving for anchovies, licorice and pickled onions. It is unlikely that your drive to the hospital will be a high-speed red-light-busting comedy of errors with a police escort. Odds are on that your wife won't be pushed down the hospital corridor on a wheely bed while you run alongside clutching her hand and declaring your undying love. Women don't always give birth with their feet up in stirrups and, I'm sorry to disappoint you, but you probably won't get to wear a gown and surgical mask for the labour. Also absent will be the witty repartee between you and your wife as she grunts comically to push the baby out. I haven't yet been to a hospital, either, that lines their newborns up behind a plate-glass window for all the relatives to stare at. And if you try to light a celebratory cigar in a hospital waiting room, you'll be beaten by nurses with bedpans.

If you're looking to the TV to supply you with a paternal role model, don't bother. Dads on the box fall into one of two categories, both of which are equally ineffectual and pathetic in their own way.

On the one hand there is the **superfather**. He is the one who has an understanding smile and incredible wisdom. He solves all problems with a few paternal clichés and the family is better again. He is always in control and is always selfless and giving. Just watch any modern sitcom or check the classics like 'The Brady Bunch', 'Happy Days', 'My Three Sons', 'Skippy', 'Home Improvement', 'Seventh Heaven' or one of my favourites, 'Lost in Space', and you'll see what I'm talking about. Of course, you never see these dads make a bed, change a nappy, set the table or lose their temper.

On the other hand is the **antifather**. These dads are ridiculously inept at fathering. They have terrible relationships with their kids and treat them either as cuddly toys or with a sense of vague detachment. If you've ever seen 'Married with Children', 'The Simpsons', 'Everybody Loves Raymond', 'Malcolm in the Middle' or 'Roseanne', you'll know what I'm talking about.

But television isn't entirely to blame for this constant stream of lies. The same applies to many parenting books, particularly the big ones with lots of glossy photos. I'm not sure where exactly they take these photos, but it sure isn't planet Earth. It must be that fantasy world known as Bookland, a place of perpetual political correctness and saccharine soft focus.

In Bookland, pregnant women float about in flattering pastel outfits. They spend their days with their hands resting meaningfully on their abdomens and wearing soft, warm, contemplative expressions on their faces. Their Bookland husbands (who look like models from advertisements for precision watches or after-shave) hold their wives tenderly and stare deeply into their eyes. Bookland dads are especially good at assembling cots and capsules without losing their tempers or cricking their backs.

In Bookland, labouring women don't sweat – they merely look determined. Their serious but competent husbands support them by knowing exactly what they want and giving it to them. The women give birth to remarkably clean babies on crisp sheets *sans blood and other fluids*. Sometimes the babies don't even have umbilical cords! All is laughter and tears of joy and sincerity dripping from the intravenous bag.

Of course the stars of the Bookland fantasy are the superbabies – babies that perpetually smile, gurgle and cock their heads cutely like puppies. Their eyes are alert, their skin is perfect and their heads are the way heads should be. Incredibly, their nappies are totally devoid of any unsightly substances. (Then again, I suppose we should be grateful. I have actually seen one DVD that showed a fair dinkum chock-full nappy being changed. No special effects. It was the real deal. That was an experience I could have done without.)

It isn't like this, either. The books lied too.

So as you walk the parental road, try not to dwell too much on what happens on the TV or in books – in some books, anyway.

That will only get you into trouble.

## CONGRATULATIONS

So, you're going to be a dad.

Congratulations. Have a cigar. Take the day off work. Celebrate by going to the pub and having a few with your mates. But (and I don't mean to spoil the moment here) exactly *why* should *you* be congratulated? No offence now, but what exactly have you done that is worthy of all this back-patting, huh? To be blunt, you had sex. That's all you've done. Chipped in a few sperm. This is why fatherhood has been described as a moment of male pleasure followed by nine months of female agony.

This idea was conveyed quite succinctly in a bizarre foreign film I saw late one night a few years ago on SBS – the title of which has now disappeared from memory, along with the content of most of my secondary education. In one particular scene, an angry woman yells at her husband in brash Portuguese:

'*What does being a father mean to you? But one second!*'

No, she wasn't criticising him for being a premature ejaculator. She was saying that to the husband, fatherhood was merely a side effect of a brief moment of sexual pleasure. Ron Howard's perceptive and terrific film, *Parenthood*, makes a similar comment. In it, Keanu Reeves says to Dianne Wiest in brash American:

*'You know ... you need a licence to buy a dog or drive a car. Hell, you need a licence to catch a fish. But they'll let any ... asshole be a father.'*

A razor-sharp truism like this hits you right between the eyes. To become a teacher, it took me four years of university study. To drive a car, I took lessons and had to pass both theoretical and practical tests. To be a father, however, all I needed was an erection, my wife and a few glasses of wine.

This logic seems backward to me, considering that becoming a dad is infinitely more important and significant than learning about verbs or knowing how far away from a stop-sign you can park your car. Any man with a working appendage can become a biological parent. But becoming a good dad takes considerably more time and effort than a simple sperm donation. That was the easy part. All the hard work – and a lot of fun – lie ahead of you.

You don't suddenly start wearing the 'Dad cap' on the day your child is born. Don't wait that long to start working on becoming a father. If you keep waiting for the 'right time', it will never come. You'll end up like the guy in that old ad: *'Do you remember last week how you said that next week you'd play with your kids? It's next week.'*

Even worse, you could end up like the dad in the classic Harry Chapin song 'Cats in the Cradle', who was always too busy to spend time with his son. One day he woke up and realised that his son had grown up, but by then it was too late. This is a great song, one which constantly inspires me to spend time with my children. I must admit, though, that I have never quite fathomed exactly what the cat was doing in the cradle in the first place, to say nothing of the concerns raised by the possibility of spreading toxoplasmosis.

Anyway, I'm sidetracking. Back to the heavy stuff.

Being a dad – being a *good* dad – is really important. It is a huge responsibility and a mammoth commitment. And it doesn't start tomorrow. It starts the moment you find out your wife is pregnant. It starts while your baby is still a mere cluster of cells in the womb. It's vital that you get your head together early in the piece and establish good patterns in fathering. So if you want to be a good dad – an involved dad – start *now*.

Congratulations on having been given the privilege and responsibility of becoming a father. But if you want to smoke the cigar, earn the right.

CHAPTER TWO

# PREGNANCY

*'They've got to get themselves from being a
single cell with only a touch of DNA for good luck to
being a whole person complete with a full set of
functioning body parts. Now that's what I call
an achievement.'*

## SUGAR AND SPICE...

Many people have a gift for asking stupid questions. For
example, on your birthday, when they ask you if you feel any
older. Or on the return from your honeymoon, when they ask
you if you are enjoying married life. Or when your wife says,
'What do you think of my new skirt?'

Stupid.

Being in the baby-making game does not exclude you from
such wanton conversational stupidity. For example, the question

that I was constantly asked during each of Meredith's pregnancies was, 'What do you think you're having – a boy or a girl?'

I think this is a stupid question for two reasons. Firstly, your child's sex is something of a lucky dip. You get what you get and there is simply no way of intuitively perceiving whether it is going to be a boy or a girl. (Sure, there may be a genetic disposition in your family, like friends of mine whose family line produced only boys for ninety-nine years. And some couples apparently take steps to try to manipulate the sex of their child, like eating a bag of lemons before conceiving under a full moon while facing south and reciting *The Canterbury Tales*. But, for most people, the sex of their child is an unknown.)

Secondly, it doesn't matter what you *think* anyway. You can *think* whatever you like and even *hope* whatever you like but ultimately this has no bearing on whether you're having a boy or a girl. You can *think* your wife is going to give birth to a slab of camembert cheese if you like and it still won't make a fig of difference.

So the question is a stupid one. However, it does lead to the more interesting question of whether or not you should find out the sex of your unborn child.

By the time your wife has an ultrasound, the trained eye of the radiographer will be able to pick out subtleties in the scan (i.e. the presence or absence of a penis) that will indicate to them – with pretty good, but not flawless, accuracy – the sex of your child. They will usually ask if you want to know.

We decided *not* to find out. We liked the excitement and suspense of not knowing. We were happy to wait till the big day itself when the doctor would say to us, 'Congratulations Mr and Mrs Downey, it's a ...' It felt to us somehow, that *not* knowing was more traditional, the way births have been for centuries, and that somehow appealed to us.

I only have a few friends who found out the sex of their child beforehand. One wanted to know because she wanted to deck out the nursery and start buying clothes in appropriate colours.

('Gender stereotyping!' I screamed at her and made a mental note to buy her unborn daughter a toy bulldozer for her first birthday.) Another wanted to know because she already had four sons – she desperately wanted a daughter and couldn't bear the suspense. If she was going to be 'disappointed' she wanted to deal with the 'disappointment' earlier rather than later (although how anyone could be 'disappointed' with a healthy baby – boy or girl – is beyond me). Another wanted to know so they could pick a name. And another friend found out – even though she didn't want to – when the radiographer slipped up while looking at a scan and said, 'Oh look, he's sucking his thumb!'

Anyway, have a chat with your wife about this and work out what you want to do.

But while I'm on the topic of stupid parenting questions, people still ask me as the father of three daughters if I am desperate for a son. Well, the answer is no, I'm not. I like having girls. At least they don't shoot jet-streams of pee into your face while you're changing their nappy. Besides, everyone knows that girls are made of sugar and spice and all things nice, whereas boys are made of frogs and snails and puppy-dog tails, which is really quite disgusting when you come to think about it.

I love being the dad of three girls and only foresee a few problems arising from this situation. I know that when my young, precious, naive, innocent girls start to go out on dates with spotty, hormonal boys with panel vans, I will have heartburn because I will remember what *I* used to do when *I* went out on dates with young, precious, naive, innocent girls. But I have already started making plans for this eventuality. I figure that when a boy comes knocking, I'll solve the problem by answering the door naked while holding my electric nail gun. That should sort the wheat from the chaff.

And I hope that by the time my daughters want to get married, our society will have lost its medieval assumption that the father of the bride has to pay for the wedding. Because if it hasn't, the only wedding presents my daughters will get from me will be a ladder and a suitcase each.

On the other hand, I wouldn't have minded having a boy, either. We could have done macho stuff together, like chopping down trees and painting murals on the side of his panel van. And I would have looked forward to the day of his marriage because it sure wouldn't have been me who'd be paying for it. Everyone knows that's the father of the bride's responsibility.

## INTERNAL GROWTH

Much of the kerfuffle surrounding this whole *childbirth thang* is directed at the mums and, to a lesser extent, us dads. Much thought, the pages of many books and websites and hours of DVD are directed at all the emotional, social, physical and psychological changes that we parents will need to make in taking on our destined roles in life. This is to say nothing of all the parental – and if you're really unlucky, *grand*-parental – advice that will be coming your way.

You will be busy trying to adjust mentally to fatherhood, you will be flat-chat trying to baby-proof your home, and you will be exhausted from shopping for all the necessities. But in the midst of all this business and self-indulgence, we can sometimes begin to forget the star of the show: the baby.

If you think *you've* got problems trying to get your stuff together in only nine months, imagine how the baby feels. They've got to get themselves from being a single cell with only a touch of DNA for good luck to being a whole person complete with a full set of functioning body parts. Now *that's* what I call an achievement.

So let's put things back in perspective a bit. The last time we mentioned the baby, the sperm had just connected with the ovum up there in the Fallopian tube and it had started its nine-month journey towards birth into the outside world. But what happens in the interim? How does it grow? When does it grow? What does it look like?

I initially had no idea about this. Up to the point when Meredith first said to me those memorable words, 'You're going to be a dad,' I really knew very little about what actually went on in the uterus, or 'womb' (a word I have always disliked. It sounds too goofy for such an important part of the body and makes me think of the noise made by a returning boomerang – *womb womb womb womb womb*). Nor did I really care. When you're at high school studying biology, things like that seem fairly low on the agenda.

With the birth of our first child imminent I consulted a few textbooks from my university days, but the big technical words were enough to drive me back into ignorance. The same applied for the hand-drawn sketches I saw on the overhead projector screen at birth classes. Then, only two months before my first daughter was born, I came across some awe-inspiring photos by acclaimed photographer Lennart Nilsson revealing the previously hidden world of the womb. Suddenly, a great light bulb flashed somewhere above my head. The veil of ignorance was lifted and the miracle of life became clear at last.

So for all of you unversed in the biological intricacies of pregnancy, here is the layman's version:

Mr Tadpole swims down the tunnel and ... no, no, just kidding.

Once the sperm and ovum have combined, the sex of your child has been determined, depending on whether the sperm was an X sperm (girl) or a Y sperm (boy). The chromosomes and genes within the sperm and ovum have also set all the genetic information. Even at this initial stage, the length of your child's fingers, the shape of their eyes, the arrangement of their teeth, the colour of their nasal hair and even the diseases they will inherit have all been decided and blueprinted into the growth sequence of the cells. This genetic program can be dominated by the features and traits of you or your wife or any of your ancestors. However, this does not explain why most babies look like Winston Churchill when they are born.

Within a day of fertilisation the nucleus will split, and continue to split again and again in the beginning of an exponential growth process. This microscopic dot is at this point called (rather unromantically) a *blastocyst*. It will begin to move south down the Fallopian tube on a three-day journey to the uterus, where it will bob around for a while looking for a cosy spot to 'dig in'. It is choosy about this, and may take up to three days before it comes across a satisfactory spot to set up camp. Once it implants, conception has officially occurred and the Beta hCG hormone will be produced, signalling to the mother that she is pregnant. Once implanted, the blastocyst moves into its next stage of development, that of being an embryo.

The embryo will then continue to split and grow until, at about the one-week mark, it will closely resemble a tiny sea anemone. It will sprout and mutate in many different directions before it even vaguely begins to look human. Two weeks from conception it will look like a reject from a seafood platter from your favourite coastal restaurant, and at about the one-month mark like that hideous beast from *Alien*, complete with seahorse-like tail and elongated head.

All the time, this fleshy blob will be developing a brain, nerves, bones, blood vessels, muscles, intestines, a heart and massive vocal chords (for late-night screaming). Six weeks after fertilisation, arms and legs will start to appear and a tiny heart will start beating at 150 beats a minute. Fingers start to grow. The lens, cornea and iris of the eye start to take shape. By the end of the third month, the embryo will have graduated to the dizzy heights of being a *foetus*. You could hold this foetus in the palm of your hand, although it would weigh as much as a few cracker biscuits. It even looks human – although I certainly wouldn't want to bump into one on a dark night.

And that's your child. Minuscule, yes. A little weird-looking, yes. But give it time. It still has six months to go.

*the baby's wastes leave through a separate channel down
the same cord ...*

During these months the foetus will float in warm, salty fluid
in a cocoon called the amniotic sac, inside the mother's uterus.
Being in an aquatic environment raises certain puzzling
questions, don't you think? For example, if I lived in a fluid-filled
sac, I would have several problems. Firstly, going to the toilet in
the same fluid that was in my mouth would not be conducive to
my good health. Secondly, have you ever tried eating underwater?

Then again, none of these problems would matter, because I'd
drown after a minute anyway.

So you have to ask yourself:

- How does the foetus breathe?
- How does the foetus get food?
- How does the foetus get rid of its waste?

In actual fact, the foetus (or baby, if you like) does not use its
mouth at all for oxygen or food consumption, and it doesn't use
its bum for waste expulsion. This is a good thing, because if it
did, just imagine the mess in there! The secret lies in technology
developed by NASA in their Space Shuttle program. Astronauts
walking in space use a hollow, hose-like tether called an

*umbilical cord* to receive all their necessary life-support requirements from the mother-ship. Women have taken this technology on board and now utilise it in their wombs.

The mother breathes air and eats food, and all the good stuff necessary for life is absorbed from these things into her bloodstream. The nutrients are transferred to the baby through a halfway station where the amniotic sac and the uterine wall meet. This is called the *placenta*. Although in its sac, the baby has its own blood supply and there is negligible exchange of blood itself. All the life-support materials (oxygen, vitamins, carbohydrates, minerals, etc.) soak through the placenta and travel down the umbilical cord straight into the baby's blood supply. Other things that can travel down the umbilical cord are nicotine, alcohol, garlic and some television frequencies. The baby's wastes leave through a separate channel down the same cord.

One interesting and exciting feature of all this growth is that as the baby gets bigger, it starts doing stuff. It sucks its thumb. It dreams (although one wonders what it dreams about, given its limited life experiences). It starts to move around. It turns, it kicks, it punches, it stretches. Basically, it's looking for a way out of there.

*to feel their child kick is a real thrill ...*

For most dads, getting to feel their child kick is a real thrill which makes them realise for the first time that there really is a little person in there. Most babies, however, have a sixth sense, so that even if they kick more than Jackie Chan, they freeze up as soon as their father puts his hand out to feel them.

## HERE'S TO HER HEALTH!

Since the baby is developing and growing inside the mother, it stands to reason that the health and general wellbeing of the mother will have a direct effect on the health and wellbeing of the baby. In short, it is important that the mother stays healthy during the pregnancy.

Now I know this is the twenty-first century, so in no way do I wish to imply that you are in charge of your wife's health. She is a free spirit, an adult who makes her own decisions. But while she is responsible for her health, it's good to know things that you can do to help.

In terms of diet, a good range of fresh food is essential to provide both mother and baby with all the necessary vitamins, proteins, carbohydrates, minerals and fats. Don't try to exist on junk food or takeaway all the time. She is getting super-sized enough without junk food adding to the situation.

Drugs have a direct impact on the unborn. If you ever go to the chemist for supplies, always inform them that your supplies are for a pregnant woman, and read the manufacturer's directions on the side of the box. You will be surprised at how many everyday drugs, from worm tablets to antihistamines, are 'not suitable for pregnant women'. (And speaking of worms and germs and things, she should also stay away from raw meat and cat and dog faeces because of a disease called toxoplasmosis. It will no doubt be a great disappointment to your wife to discover that she will have to stay away from pet excrement for several months, but hey, we all have to make sacrifices.)

While alcohol may be considered by some to be generally conducive to good health, in terms of the unborn it too needs to be consumed in sensible moderation. (Many people would say it shouldn't be consumed at all.) Pregnant women can have occasional small amounts of alcohol, assuming of course that it's a glass of wine, not a schooner-sized top-shelf cocktail of rocket fuel. Like I said, alcohol goes straight through the placenta and into the baby, and your wife probably doesn't want a drunk baby singing karaoke inside her. So if you and your wife are in the habit of having a drink together or are connoisseurs of fine wines, perhaps you can help by not tempting her by cracking a bottle of Grange over dinner.

The same applies to smoking. Smoking is *really* bad news for an unborn because the baby can't get all the oxygen it needs. Cigarettes are packed full of junk which your baby most definitely does not want to know about, including ammonia, nicotine, tar, formaldehyde, nickel, cadmium, carbon monoxide and even poisons (arsenic and cyanide) and radioactive compounds. This can lead to a whole panoply of problems, the least of which is stunted foetal development, which in turn leads to reduced birth weight. Smoking also increases the potential for miscarriage, deformity and, in severe cases, the death of the baby soon after birth. The child of a smoking mother is twice as likely to die of Sudden Infant Death Syndrome (SIDS), and this risk doubles again if the father smokes. Cigarette packets are not kidding when they state, 'Smoking harms your unborn baby'. And to top it off, if your baby does make it through the pregnancy it could be born with yellow-stained fingers and a hacking cough.

If you and your wife both smoke and she decides to give up, respect her decision and support her by not smoking near her. And don't forget that *passive smoking* is also dangerous. So if you smoke and your wife doesn't, don't smoke while she's trapped in the car or in an unventilated room with you. Maybe you could even give up yourself?

Then again, that's easy for me to say – I've never smoked. In fact, I'm one of those smug, self-righteous bastards who, when people say to me, 'Do you mind if I smoke?' replies, 'Go ahead … I don't mind getting cancer just so you can feel relaxed.'

But hey … that's just me.

## DECISIONS, DECISIONS

The thing about pregnancy is that the baby won't stay in there forever. It has to come out sometime. When it does come out, the process is called *labour*, which in my *Macquarie Dictionary* is defined as 'work, especially of a hard or fatiguing kind'. This is another great euphemism; a word like *agony* is probably more appropriate to describe the process of childbirth, but it doesn't have that certain ring to it.

During the term of pregnancy, you and your wife will need to make some decisions about how and where the labour and birthing process is to take place. This is because, like many other good things in life – overseas trips and theatre parties, for example – you just can't turn up on the day. You need to book.

Some couples find hospitals impersonal and disempowering, so they opt for having their babies at home. It is perhaps more comfortable to give birth in familiar surroundings, and although the birth is usually supervised by a midwife, there is minimal medical intervention. Women have been having babies at home for thousands of years, and even today home births are the norm for millions of women around the world. While not too many Western women take up this option today, it is still a reasonable choice for a healthy woman who has had an uncomplicated pregnancy.

Home births only account for a few per cent of all births in Australia, and it looks like that figure will only get smaller in the future. Health insurance companies do not cover home births, so you will have to pay the midwife's fees yourself, making it more expensive than a hospital birth. In addition, recent changes in the world of liability insurance mean that it is difficult (read: 'next to impossible') for midwives to get insurance cover themselves. And for fear of getting sued, fewer midwives are willing to put their necks on the line.

Some people still do it. My sister-in-law had an unassisted home birth and thought it was a fabulous experience. If you're the sort of person who can handle this, good-o. But I wouldn't do it in a pink fit.

We decided against a home-birth for three reasons:

- we didn't like the possibility of neighbours dropping in for a cup of tea in the middle of it all;
- the whole idea scared me to death. We wanted the resources of a fully equipped multi-million-dollar hospital, complete with expert personnel and a doctor who had done it thousands of times before and had lots of impressive certificates hanging on his or her surgery wall; and
- we had just had new carpets put down in the house.

Other people opt for birth centres, which are more 'homey' than hospitals. These centres have a more relaxed atmosphere, a less sterile decor, and are more accepting of non-interventionist birthing methods. They are run by midwives and often are a separate unit of a hospital so staff have access to additional medical support if necessary.

The majority of women still go to a hospital. Ideally your hospital should be near your home, so you can reach it relatively quickly without having to break speed limits or drive on footpaths. The most fantastic hospital in the world is no good if it is on the other side of the city. You'll only end up having the baby in the back of the car, which will be bad for the upholstery and will lower its resale value.

Part of your choice will also be dictated by your health cover. Make no mistake, childbirth can be expensive. All you have to do is look at the contents of the 'Reserved for Doctors Only' car-spaces at the hospital and notice they are all fully imported luxury coupés with GPS navigation systems to realise that there is a lot of money involved in this whole childbirth thing.

After you or your wife has phoned up the hospital to make the booking, your wife will probably have to go in for an interview, fill out forms giving personal details, and generally answer a lot of questions. The hospital will also want to know what kind of health cover she has, if any.

Your wife can go to a *public hospital* as a *public patient*, which means she gets the specialist who is on duty in the hospital at the time. As the name suggests, the facilities are public. The women there will probably share rooms and bathrooms. I have friends who wouldn't go anywhere but the local public hospital, and others who are the exact opposite. It depends on your financial situation and your expectations. Going public is the least expensive option, particularly if you have no private cover.

If you want to go private, you have a choice. Choosing a hospital is like most things – you need to shop around to find out what's best for you. Ask your friends for recommendations, talk to your family doctor, and visit some hospitals. Most hospitals have a labour-ward tour you can go on so you can fully check out the facilities.

So if you have health cover, what exactly is your wife covered for? The best thing is to get on the phone to your insurance company or visit their website and cross-reference your coverage with the hospital fees. The difference will tell you your debt level.

For the birth of Rachael, Meredith had private cover and went as a *private patient* to a *public hospital*. This meant that because we had the cover, we could afford Meredith's own doctor. (See below.) But we wanted the public hospital because it was closest to our home and we were familiar with it, since we had been to birth classes there. The maternity ward also had a solid reputation and the staff were great. The hospital had a warm and welcoming atmosphere and it just felt right.

However, there were some things about the hospital that we weren't too happy about afterwards. During the first stage of labour, Meredith had to share one toilet with three other labouring women who were in equal need of the facility. We were all in the same large room and the curtains did little to shield us from their collective wailing and moaning. After the birth, the visiting hours were not strictly enforced so Meredith was bombarded by guests almost all day and got tired very quickly. She also shared a room with a woman who was always visited by at least ten relatives with very loud voices. To top it off, this woman had a baby who screamed *non-stop*.

So for the births of Georgia and Matilda, Meredith went as a *private patient* to a *private hospital*. We were both more confident the second and third time around and so were happy about travelling a greater distance to reach this hospital. Meredith had her own room, so she got some peace and quiet, and her own en suite, which made life a bit easier. The staff were ever-vigilant about visiting hours, too. Dads could visit anytime, but if you weren't a dad and you arrived out of visiting hours, you'd never make it past the sentry dogs and armed nurses who patrolled the corridors. In terms of cost, all up with our private cover the gap was several hundred dollars. If it wasn't for the cover, however, the births would have set us back several thousand. But that's what you pay if you want a maternity ward that serves king prawns and mudcake for dinner.

A final word of warning, however: if you decide to go to a private hospital you will need to book in quickly. Spaces are limited and they go faster than grand final tickets. Some women even book in within minutes of conception.

I kid you not.

Some questions you might like to consider when choosing a hospital are:

- What is the availability of toilets and showers?
- What are the rooms like?
- How many patients to a room?
- Do they have facilities for 'different' types of births, or do they stick to 'traditional' methods?
- What is their attitude to pain relief?
- How long do they let mothers stay to recover after the birth?
- Is there a phone available in the room for post-birth calls?
- Is there a patient rest period each day when visitors aren't allowed in?
- Do the babies sleep in the mother's room or are they in a nursery?
- What magazines do they have in the kiosk?
- Do they have a nearby emergency ward, in case a father faints and splits his head open on the concrete floor and has to be taken away for stitches?

If your wife does go as a private patient – either in a private or a public hospital – she gets to have the doctor of her choice. This specialist doctor is called an *obstetrician*. Obstetricians have a lot of letters after their name and drive convertibles with speedos that go up to 350 kilometres an hour. They usually don't work every hospital, so that may be another factor limiting your wife's choice. And like a hospital, their time is finite, so she'll have to 'book in' with them as well. Once again, this needs to be done fairly quickly.

But how do you go about choosing a doctor?

It may be that your wife already has one. But if she doesn't, she has to shop for one. I have a friend who visited four obstetricians and then chose the one she liked best. Shopping around like this offers maximum choice, but it also promises to be expensive. Don't do it unless at least one of you is an international business tycoon.

*choosing a doctor ...*

Most of my friends chose their doctor on the recommendation of other friends or their own GP. But this decision is very personal. I have another friend who wanted a female obstetrician. She said that having a male obstetrician was like having a vegetarian teach you how to barbecue ribs.

It is vital that your wife likes the doctor and feels comfortable with him or her. It is also important that you both find out the doctor's attitudes towards intervention, pain relief, birth positions, the role of the father, and so on. You don't want to discover in the delivery room that your ideas and expectations are vastly different.

Another thing you need to find out is how much you will be charged. This is *very important*. Most European cars are expensive to run, and the money comes from one place. That's right ... *you*. Once again, you should check your private health cover.

It is the obstetrician's job to monitor both mother and baby during the pregnancy and then to be there to supervise the birth and 'deliver' the baby. Part of this monitoring process involves a series of check-ups. These take place monthly, but can be every fortnight as the birth draws closer, and then every week. During these visits your wife's blood, urine, weight and blood pressure are tested. These visits also test your wife's patience, as invariably she will sit for three hours waiting for her appointment.

On several occasions I was able to go along with Meredith to her check-ups. I found this to be really beneficial, because I got to meet and know the doctor and was able to ask all the questions that were flooding my mind ('What happens if the baby is too big to get out?' 'What happens if the contractions start too early?' 'How do you find the fuel consumption of your new Subaru?'). This was also a great way to share the experience of pregnancy and helped me to prepare for what lay ahead.

On one of these occasions, the doctor put a microphoney thing (a foetal stethoscope) on Meredith's pregnant bit and she and I sat in awe, listening to the gallop of our unborn baby's heart. This was a great thrill! It really made me realise that there was a little person in there. If you can, go along to experience this.

Another thing the doctor does is calculate the expected date of birth. A normal pregnancy lasts, as you know, about nine months, although it is 'normal' for babies to be born between thirty-seven and forty-two weeks. However, the baby doesn't have a calendar in the womb and might not want to wait until the conveniently predicted ninth months to tick over before deciding to make the grand entrance. Premature babies can be born from seven months, or twenty-eight weeks, into the pregnancy.

Personally, I subscribe to the view that this whole 'due date' thing is a bit of a professional conspiracy and private prank among obstetricians. I can almost picture it. Many years ago, at the Annual Conference for Obstetricians with Flashy Cars, one obstetrician leaned across to some others and said, 'Hey guys, I've got this really great joke that we can all play on nervous expectant couples ...'

I'm not sure how they actually calculate the date, but I suspect it's done with a dart thrown onto a calendar. The doctor will probably also ask your wife to have an ultrasound to confirm the due date, as well as to check out a few other things. This will be at around the eighteen-week mark of her pregnancy.

## ULTRASOUND

There is no doubt that we live in a wonderful age of technology. We have at our disposal all sorts of fantastic gismos and whirligigs that can do all sorts of amazing and incredible things that our parents would never have believed possible.

Sadly, some of our advancements have been a big mistake and have only served to drag humanity further down into the abyss of self-destruction. These include:

- aerosol cheese;
- those things which make the water in your toilet turn blue;
- mobile phones;
- karaoke machines;
- reality television; and
- cloning.

But some of the advancements seem to have generally been quite a good idea, and quite frankly I don't know why someone didn't think of them earlier. For example:

- microsurgery;
- photocopiers with a collating function;
- caller ID;
- unbleached toilet paper;
- microwave popcorn; and, of course,
- the wonderful ultrasound machine.

It used to be that Mum and Dad had to wait for the grand debut, on the day of birth, to get their first look at Junior. These days are no longer, thanks to the marvels of modern medical technology.

Here's how it works:

You and your wife go down to the local ultrasound shop. Then you sit in the waiting room until you're called in to lie down on the ultrasound couch. This will take place at the exact moment when you're up to the climax of the 'A 747 crashed into my car ... and I survived!' story in the *Reader's Digest* from the waiting-room coffee-table.

(Before I go on, here's a useful thing to remember. For the ultrasound to work, the woman has to drink several litres of water. This is uncomfortable at the best of times, but if she has to have an ultrasound later in the pregnancy, her bladder may be only slightly larger than a walnut. When this is the case, do not under any circumstances tickle her or attempt to give her a hug or go on bushwalks near babbling brooks or waterfalls.)

Anyway, back to the couch. The radiographer will come in and probe the swollen front bit of your wife (i.e. where the baby lives) with a microphoney thing. This sends out high-frequency sound waves (hence *ultra*-sound), which are then reflected back and processed onto a television monitor for you all to see in glorious black and white.

And there you have it.

A black screen with lots of white, fuzzy, wriggling squiggles.

This is your child.

The radiographer will say amazing things to you like, 'There's Baby's arm', 'There's Baby's beating heart' and 'Baby's facing this way'. Actually, I think that they're just having a little joke with us all and that the ultrasound picture is simply a badly-tuned TV station. It reminds me of The Emperor's New Clothes. There's nothing definable on the screen, but still everybody goes, 'Yeah, wow ... I think I see a hand!' Nobody wants to be the first to say, 'I can't see a thing!' And so the myth is perpetuated.

When I saw the first ultrasound picture of Rachael, I thought Meredith was giving birth to a satellite photo of Earth. There were her legs (cumulus clouds over Sydney), her chest (low-pressure front moving north), and her head (cyclone off the coast). It's pretty exciting stuff.

And the other exciting thing about a visit to the radiographer is that not only do you get to look at the picture on the screen, but often you can even take home souvenirs of the event as well. There are two main types of souvenir. For starters, you can get snapshot 'photos' of the monitor pictures. These look like X-rays, with body-part labels so you can identify exactly what it is you are looking at. Why not start your own baby photo album – months before the birth!!

The other, and increasingly more popular, type of souvenir is the video or DVD. Yes, you can capture the entire ultrasound in laborious detail and watch it all again and again in the comfort of your own home. Imagine the hilarity when you surprise your son or daughter by playing their forty-minute ultrasound tape at their twenty-first birthday party! Won't their friends be impressed?!

Technology, of course, is always on the move and, as such, ultrasounds are also developing. Whereas ultrasounds used to be 2D black and white stills, now 3D imaging is available which provides a much more detailed picture. These coloured images are kind of spooky, looking a bit like death masks you find in old penal museums or the 3D image of a ghostly presence computerised in some pseudo-techno haunted house flick. When combined in a series of images taken one after the other, you get a '4D effect', kind of like when you draw pictures in the corners of each page in a book and then flick it to make the image appear to move. Such ultrasounds are considered of more entertainment value than medical necessity, but some parents want to start their video collection early.

In fact, I'm sure it won't be long before we see a whole new line in ultrasound marketing. How about an ultrasound-print T-shirt? Or an ultrasound fridge magnet? Why not an assortment of ultrasound postcards to send out to your friends? And why not one of those tasteful plastic domes with a replica foetus inside? All you do is shake ... and it snows!

Having an ultrasound achieves three things. First, as already mentioned, the doctor can check the estimated date of delivery. This is done by measuring the length of one of the baby's bones. Invariably the due date is quite different to the one supplied to you originally. (And simply adds weight to my previously mentioned theory regarding 'due dates'.)

Second, the doctor gets to make sure everything is OK and all the baby's bits are where they're supposed to be.

Third, you can tell how many babies are in there waiting to come out. Mathematically, odds are that it is only going to be one. But if you can count four legs, either your wife is going to give birth to a horse or you're going to be the father of twins.

You have about a 1 in 86 chance of having twins, a 1 in 8000 chance of having triplets, a 1 in 650 000 chance of having quads and a 1 in 400 billion chance of having septuplets. If you can count seven or more pairs of legs, you'd better sell your car and buy a mini-bus, because you're going to need it.

And just be thankful that you aren't Feodor Vassilyev, a Russian peasant whose wife (according to Guinness World Records) gave birth to sixteen pairs of twins, seven sets of triplets and four sets of quadruplets – 69 children in all, and a world-record-holding feat of reproduction.

## LIFE'S LITTLE CHANGES

It can sometimes be hard to come to terms with all the little changes that arrive with pregnancy. They may be subtle at first, but as the months inexorably tick away, things will start seeming 'different'. You will notice that your wife is beginning to ... *transform*.

There are hormonal changes to consider. Her body is chock-full of progesterone and oestrogen and so she may exhibit mood swings as variable as tropical weather conditions. For example, in answer to the simple and straightforward question, 'Would you like a cuppa?' you could get a simple, 'Yes please' or 'No thanks'. However, you could also get a teary, 'That's the most beautiful thing you've ever said to me,' or an aggressive, 'Don't *patronise* me! I can make my own tea!'

While most pregnant women may not quite fit the weepy or cranky stereotype bandied about on television sitcoms all the time, a ride on the mood roller-coaster at some point in their pregnancy is not uncommon for many women. Other side effects on the pregnancy smorgasbord may include cravings, headaches, clumsiness, heartburn, fluid retention, high blood pressure, cramps, vagueness and tiredness. Kind of makes you want to be pregnant, doesn't it?

Of course there's still the aforementioned morning sickness to consider. And what can you, as a caring twenty-first-century man, do to alleviate the horrible nausea? I've heard of different remedies, such as dry toast, back rubs, glucose, ginger, steam inhalation, frequent small meals, lots of fluids, herbal tea and a clove of garlic hung around the neck. Some people swear by iron tablets or saline drips, and I've even heard of one remedy involving a cat, a battery and a tube of toothpaste, but in the interests of good taste I think it best I don't elaborate on this.

Other than this there's not a whole heap you can do. Morning sickness will happen when it wants to and you can't stop it. However, you can help not to make it worse than it already is. Make her a cup of tea to drink before she gets out of bed. Don't bait your fishing line in front of her. When cooking, avoid fatty and spicy foods and strong or aromatic herbs, and if serving chicken, don't give her the parson's nose. Most importantly, if she looks green, don't stand between her and the bathroom.

One increasingly obvious change you will notice is that the baby is getting bigger and bigger and bigger inside her. Using basic dimensional mathematics, it is easy to deduce that all your wife's other internal bits and pieces have less and less and less room. This causes decreased bladder size. In short, it means that your own lengthy interludes in the bathroom reading the local paper or the latest Phantom comic will have to be cut short. It also means that epic car journeys may need to be re-thought. And whatever you do, *don't* say, 'Can you just hang on for another half an hour?' A woman with a bladder the size of a walnut should not be messed with.

On average your wife will gain around eleven kilos. Interestingly, only about a third of this gain is the weight of the baby. The other weight is made up from increases in fluids (blood, amniotic fluid), fat, the uterus and the placenta. The most obvious sign of this gain is that your wife won't be able to fit into those old denim jeans or her favourite dress anymore. Coincidentally, it's around this time that you notice a lot of your own clothes go missing, particularly big and baggy jumpers, T-shirts and sloppy joes. It shouldn't take Sherlock Holmes to work out who the culprit is. On top of this, you will probably need to break out the credit card and go buying a new range of fashion marquees, also referred to as 'maternity wear'.

Another obvious change is the increase in size of your wife's breasts. This can begin early in her pregnancy but usually really kicks in during the last trimester. The change is caused by the mammary glands in her breasts getting ready for all the hard work ahead of them. In fact, they can increase in size by up to two cups, which according to the measuring bowl in our kitchen is about a quarter of a litre. But although your wife's breasts are swollen and inviting, they are probably quite sore. While you might be boggle-eyed in the presence of her invitingly engorged bosom, it does not necessarily follow that she will enjoy or even allow gropings on your part. So keep your damn hands to yourself.

While these physical changes can make life awkward, they are not always as paralysing as television mums would have us believe. (See Chapter One.) Pregnancy and childbirth are normal and healthy. A pregnant woman is not 'sick' and shouldn't be treated as such. Having said that, your wife certainly won't be as nimble as she used to be. Due to the new weight distribution, sore backs are common. Many everyday activities can become increasingly awkward and even painful for her. Sleeping becomes quite difficult as, in addition to the less than convenient new shape of her body, she has to cope with such troublesome maladies as heartburn, increased heart rate, shortness of breath and a frequent need to go to the toilet. Sleeping on her back or stomach can become quite uncomfortable and so the side becomes a favoured position, which offers some relief from the massive weight on her front. In fact, towards the end of the pregnancy, nearly all sleeping positions can be quite uncomfortable, so do all you can to help out. Stuff pillows in all the right places for support. You can purchase an extensive range of full body pillows, maternity pillows and pillow wedges which are less cumbersome than trying to build a pillow castle in your bed with ordinary pillows.

There are plenty of other things you can do to make your wife's life a little easier, but don't treat her as though she's a porcelain doll you expect to sit in a corner for nine months. Instead, do more than your 'fair share' of the cooking, cleaning, washing and ironing. Give her back rubs on demand. Tie her shoelaces for her. Avoid using words like 'dromedary' and 'orca' in her presence. Treat her to breakfast in bed. Be understanding if her aching body or nausea interfere with social engagements. In short, be totally superhuman.

## MORE ON SEX

Ah, yes – this is what caused all this fuss in the first place. And you want more?

When we announced to the world that Meredith was pregnant, one of our friends sidled up to me with a sincere look on his face and said with a voice of utmost concern, 'Mate, there goes your sex life for the next year.'

Up to this point I had not even considered this as being a problem. But once it was brought to my attention, I broke out in the cold sweat of ignorance. Did this *really* mean that my wife and I would not be engaging in that which was normal and healthy in our marriage?

What a relief it was to find that just because my wife was pregnant, she did not immediately enter sexual quarantine. In fact, far from it (but that's another story, and quite frankly one you'll never hear). Sex is possible and normal during pregnancy. And by the way, if you think your pregnant wife is off-limits because your whopping great fertility organ will be a physical threat to the baby, I only have one thing to say to you: *Don't flatter yourself.*

Having said that, however, there are a few commonsense things to keep in mind. As I said earlier, during pregnancy the female body goes through incredible changes. Because one of these is hormonal, you may find that your wife's previous voracious sexual appetite has dimmed somewhat. In short, she may not 'feel like it'. It may not be as frequent as in 'the good old days'. (Of course, the opposite may also apply.) It is important that you come to terms with this and understand all the changes her body is trying to cope with. She definitely does not need you giving her the 'nudge-nudge, wink-wink' treatment.

And even when you do engage in sex or sexual play, there are physical limitations. You will find that it's not as acrobatic as it once might have been. Swinging from light fittings, wholesale destruction of bedroom furniture, athletic Greco–Roman wrestling positions and anything to do with the Karma Sutra or yoga are definitely out. You will need to be a little more creative in terms of getting the pieces of the puzzle to fit together comfortably, if you get my drift. If you need some sensitivity-training in this area, try strapping a beanbag and a couple of house bricks around your stomach and then see how you feel about sex.

Of course, all women are different. It's important that the two of you discuss your sexuality together and tell each other how you are feeling. It's important that you are understanding and supportive of her. Sex is a good and normal part of relationships, but pregnancy can temporarily alter the normal pattern.

# OF OPOSSUMS AND MEN

I feel sorry for the male opossum. There he is, enjoying *coitus opossumatus* in a comfortable branch of his favourite tree, when only thirteen days later – that's right, count 'em – his mate gives birth to an opossumette. This probably accounts for the high incidence of stomach ulcers among male opossums.

Luckily, we non-marsupials are given a little more leeway. Nine months is quite a decent period in which to get ready for our new stations in life. But this does not mean that parents-to-be have nine months to relax and party on. Use this valuable time to work hard in preparing for the arrival of your humanette. And believe me, it *is* hard work. Spend your time wisely. Read Chapter Three.

Don't be fooled into thinking that this time will go slowly. We're not as fortunate as the African elephant, which has a gestation period of about twenty-one months. African elephant dads certainly have no excuse if *they're* not ready for life on the plains with a young pachyderm.

As I mentioned in Chapter One, it's common in the early stages of their wife's pregnancy for dads-to-be to feel a bit disorientated. Already everyone who knows you're going to be a dad has started treating you differently, your sex life has entered the realm of the dinosaurs, you've nobly stood by your wife in steering clear of gin and tonics, you've stared in dismay at your bank balance, your wife has vomited in the bathroom – and it's only been twenty-four hours since you heard the news.

Welcome to pregnancy!

But don't worry. Unlike the opossum, you still have several months to get used to it.

# CHAPTER THREE

# TIME TO GET READY

*'A deathly silence fell over the room. We moved on, but none of us were ever the same again.'*

## FACING THE FACTS

To start you on the road of fatherhood, let me bring you back down to earth with a sobering thought. I warned you at the start of this book but I'll say it again: Life as you have known it is over.

*Finito. Ende. Kaput.*

So long. Farewell. *Auf Wiedersehen.* Goodbye.

Gone. History. Jurassic.

Your life as a dad will be totally different from anything you have known. It sure changed my life. It may come as a surprise to you, but I haven't always driven a Tarago and I never used to leave parties at 10 pm. I haven't always hung out at the wading pool at the local swim centre, and my idea of a great night hasn't always been takeaway hamburgers in front of *Finding Nemo*.

But that was *before*.

Get used to the fact that you can't be a CWOC (couple with one child) or a CASK (couple and several kids) while trying to live like a DINK (double income, no kids) or a SINK (single income, no kids). The lifestyles, responsibilities, roles and daily routines of CWOCs/CASKs and DINKs/SINKs are totally different, opposed and mutually exclusive. If you try to live like a DINK when you're a CWOC, you will find it very frustrating and exhausting. If you try to live like a SINK when you're a CASK, you will find it impossible. You'll end up wishing you were still a WANKA (without any new kids anyway).

What I'm talking about is your use of time. You used to have a lot of it to throw around and please yourself with. Game of golf this afternoon? *Sure!* Beer after work? *Yes!* Knock off another novel in the hammock? *Great!* A quick surf? *Certainly!* A late movie? *Why not?* House renovations? *Nothing better to do!*

But not anymore. The responsibility of active fathering demands your time. Parenting takes time. Your child needs your time. There are no shortcuts or ways around this.

There are three main areas in which you'll need to deliberately do some basic time management over the next twelve months. First, there are the *coming months of pregnancy*. You and your wife will be busy getting ready for the arrival of a new person in the house. This is an especially time-consuming operation, involving an almost infinite list of 'things to do'. But the better you prepare now, the better it will be for you later on.

Second, there is the expected time of arrival, often referred to as the *due date* or *mission improbable*. You need to attack your calendars and palm-pilots and diaries with a thick black pen (but not your palm-pilot) in the weeks surrounding this elusive date, since babies don't usually follow adult timetables. They can come early. They can come late.

In fact, they probably will.

It is extremely important that you are available and on-call when that giant roulette wheel in the sky drops the ball and your baby starts heading out of the womb. And you need to be around in the weeks that follow. This is a tumultuous time, when a heavy work and/or social schedule will not help the situation.

Let your employer know the due date and find out their expectations regarding your taking a few days off at zero notice. If your work allows you any flexibility, avoid loading up the weeks around the due date. (Don't book interstate holidays, golf days or expensive theatre seats around this time, either.) A lot of my friends took their long-service leave or annual holidays so they could be around during those crucial first weeks at home. Some employers are even so egalitarian as to offer paternity leave.

And third, in the longer term, your *new family life* will be time-consuming. Coming home from work at unthinkable hours, commitments on every night of the week (training, TAFE/uni, gym, movies, rehearsals, beer-drinking, visiting mates, meetings, etc.), and raging on weekends until the wee hours, will leave you with very little time to be a father (or a husband, for that matter).

You may have already come across the expression 'quality time'. The theory behind this is that you spend intensive time with your child, focused on them. This could be cuddling them, singing to them, taking them for a walk, talking to them. Such 'quality time' is important, as long as it is not misused. You can not make up for working ridiculous hours and never being at home by grabbing a desperate thirty minutes of book reading once every blue moon.

Instead you also need to think in terms of 'quantity time'. This is simply the very domestic act of hanging around the house and spending time with your family doing everyday stuff. In short, your child simply needs you to be around. I'm not suggesting that you leave your job and spend twenty-four hours a day with your family. Obviously there'll be times when things are hectic and work demands much of your attention. In some ways, it is an unavoidable part of our contemporary work ethic. But as a general rule, your family needs to be placed up high on the priority agenda.

So sit down with your wife and talk over your weekly schedules. Basically, once the baby comes you'll need to spend a lot of time at home. This won't happen magically of its own accord. It takes deliberate thought and effort on your part to establish new time schedules, and it just might mean you'll have to toss some things in.

It all sounds pretty bleak, doesn't it? Well, it's not. It's just different.

At first, you'll still be able to operate pretty much as normal. Newborns are portable and generally sedate, so you can take them with you to dinner parties or soccer matches without too much hassle. Later, when they're older and outings become more difficult, you and your wife can work as a team and take turns in looking after the baby while the other goes out. Things like sports, part-time study, social gatherings, rehearsals, club meetings and so on can all be juggled in moderation. Babysitters,

*no set time for when a pregnant woman has to leave work ...*

relatives and clucky friends can also give you the opportunity to go out together.

Sure, you do lose some freedom. But there're no freebies in this world, and that's the price you pay for the privilege and pleasure of being a dad.

By the way, when I said that it's not really that bleak, I was only kidding.

## WORKING IN A COALMINE...

Some jobs are just plain hard to do when there's another person living and growing inside your skin. If your wife is a judo instructor, for example, she will find it increasingly difficult to fulfil her work commitments. Likewise if she is a professional netball player, coal miner, mud-wrestler or police officer.

Also, she may find it hard if she works in a place where she is on her feet all day or has to run around town at top speeds. As the pregnancy progresses, she will tend to get tired more quickly. Aching muscles will come with increasing regularity. Eventually there will come a time when work will have to go. Most bosses don't want their employees having babies whilst on company grounds; the carpet shampoo is just too expensive to take the risk.

When Meredith was pregnant with Rachael, she was working for a government department on the other side of the CBD. That meant she had a considerable peak-hour bus journey, followed by another bus journey and then a good walk before she actually reached her workplace. As the months went by, getting to work became harder and harder for her. First, there was the daily terror of a potential vomiting-on-a-crowded-bus situation. But she got over that. Then later on, when Meredith got physically bigger, she found that chivalry was unfortunately dead on many an occasion. She often stood the entire journey with baby kicking, bladder bursting and back aching. Sometimes, if she was particularly uncomfortable, she would say in a loud voice to no one in particular, 'Excuse me, I'm pregnant. Would you mi–?'

She never once finished her sentence. It was incredible how chivalrous people suddenly became!

Meredith nutted out the agony of work and the horrors of public transport for seven months before deciding that enough was enough. However, there is no set time for when a pregnant woman has to leave work. It's usually up to how she feels, although I suspect that the dark shadow of mortgage repayments puts a heavy strain on many couples these days. Some women enjoy the luxury of being able to leave work as soon as they 'hear the news'. Others, for reasons either of finance or job commitment, bash it out for as long as they can.

The choices regarding leaving work are not extensive. Women can either leave their positions for good, or they can take maternity leave. There is a range of maternity leave regulations and variations, so your wife should consult her relevant personnel department, her state government's industrial relations department, or her union or industry body for the specifics that apply to her employment situation. (While it is illegal to discriminate in the workplace against a pregnant woman, there may be specific limitations in relation to her job; for example, if she works with hazardous substances or is a commercial pilot or air traffic controller.) No matter which way you go, your family income will be affected, so be prepared to go without two incomes for a couple of months before the expected time of delivery.

You and your wife also need to discuss post-birth work arrangements. A few years ago, this would not have been an issue. Social convention dictated that pregnant women left the workforce forever, to be sucked into the vortex of domestic life. But then came the revolution. The air is still thick with the ash of burnt bras, and social convention no longer dictates that a pregnant woman is doomed to premature career death.

So the dual-career couple is now commonplace in our society, but this presents another problem. What does the dual-career couple do when the baby comes along? You can't just leave a newborn in its crib for the day while you both go off to work. Nor is it likely that either of you can tuck it under your arm and take it to work with you.

That's right. Someone has to look after the baby.

How you resolve this issue will be influenced by a number of factors, such as how flexible your workplaces are, how big your mortgage repayments are, which of you earns the most money, your attitudes to breast- and/or bottle-feeding, how much cash you have in the bank, your convictions regarding full-time parenting, the willingness and capability of well-meaning nearby grandparents who are itching to get in on some serious grandparent time, and which of you has the stronger will.

There are all sorts of possibilities and solutions open to you. Meredith and I have a fairly traditional approach. Despite having a university degree and a career path, Meredith decided to leave work to take up the position as Mother and Domestic Manager with a new but rapidly growing business called The Downey Family. Doing it this way isn't so hot financially, but it does make for a secure and consistent home environment, which we both value.

There are many other approaches available to you, depending on how flexible or innovative you want to be. The couple across the road from us take turns in working and being at home for periods of roughly one year, thus giving each of them an experience of life as a full-time parent. Of course, it doesn't make for a smooth climb up the career ladder. I also once met a couple who worked out their jobs so that they both get to experience full-time parenting and full-time work. The mum works the day shift (8 am until 4 pm) and the dad works the night shift (3 pm until 11 pm). The baby is minded for two hours in the interim. It's good for them financially, but the problem is that they only see each other as husband and wife on Sundays. This is not particularly conducive to the development of a married relationship.

Other friends I know both hold down nine-to-five jobs while the baby's grandparents play babysitters during the day. The service is free and the grandparents relish the opportunity to spend time with their grandchild.

If you both want to work nine-to-five but your parents are nowhere to be found, private organisations and your local council also run family day care and day care centres.

Family day care is where your baby is minded in the carer's home. It provides a stable environment for your baby, with close supervision from the carer. The carer is only licensed to look after a small number of kids at a time, and the home is regularly inspected by your council to make sure it is safe and clean.

Other day care centres are larger, sometimes caring for up to forty children at a time. The advantage of these centres is that, unlike in the family day care situation, if the regular carer is sick there is still someone else available to look after your baby. Often your baby can be minded for longer hours, too. There are only two drawbacks: it's often difficult to get a place for your baby, and you have to pay for it. Waiting lists for little babies can be up to eighteen months long, because babies are more labour-intensive than your average semi-independent toddler. Babies can also be more expensive. Some private day care centres could cost you hundreds each week, depending on the number of hours your baby spends there. While some workplaces are pioneering on-site child-minding facilities, these tend to be few and far between.

Family day care is much cheaper, at just a few dollars an hour, but it can also be hard to find a place. The thing to do is to put your baby's name (if it *has* a name, but more about that later) down on the lists of childcare places and with your local council *as soon as possible*. No matter where you decide to go, check it out. All centres must be accredited by the Commonwealth Government and conform to specific carer–child ratios which are readily available on the internet. If you're given a place, go down and check out the facilities and the carers. You will very soon get a feel for the place. If, for example, there is an unfenced pond in the play area and the Carer In Charge is wearing an 'Anarchy Forever' T-shirt, you might want to try somewhere else.

If your wife does decide to go back to the paid workforce – in whatever capacity – she probably won't be doing it straight away. I mean, there's nothing stopping her from going back the day after the baby is born, if she really wants to – that is, assuming she can still walk. However, most women returning to the workforce go back usually around three to six months after the birth. By then they can walk without hobbling, their breast milk doesn't soak their blouses and people have stopped asking them, 'When are you due?'

## NESTING URGE

Science tells us that all birds have a nesting urge. In the period before they lay their eggs, they go into a frenzy of nest-making. This is so that when the eggs emerge, they will have somewhere warm and safe to stay until the chicks hatch.

All birds get the nesting urge.

All pregnant women get the nesting urge.

Now, although your wife hopefully won't be up a tree making a little basket out of twigs, cotton and mud, the nesting urge will definitely manifest itself in its own cute way. It is unavoidable. It's some kind of biological thing. In women's brains, just under the hypothalamus, there is a small gland which secretes nesting-urge hormone. When this gland starts operating, you will notice some changes in your wife … like an absence of logic, no concept of reason, and a strong desire to make major architectural changes to your home.

As a young married couple, we were fortunate to be able to live in my old family home. We decided to make a room for the baby in my old bedroom, which was modelled on Greg Brady's 'den'. All the furniture was built-in and connected at different levels: bed, cupboards, bookshelves, drawers and a desk. It was painted a groovy fire-engine red. The crowning glory was a huge, pool-hall style, rice-paper light-shade, complete with tassels, which dangled from the ceiling.

A perfect room for a baby!

Or so I thought.

I remember the day clearly. Returning from work, I pulled into the driveway and immediately knew something was awry. This was primarily because my aforementioned bedroom lay in a large, red mountain of splintered wood in the middle of the backyard.

In a daze I made my way into the house, clambering over an enormous roll of shredded carpet that I was sure wasn't there when I'd left for work that morning.

In the shell of my old room I found my excessively pregnant wife, bathed in sweat and grime, blithely chiselling sheets of old paint and wallpaper off the walls. Half the room was already stripped back to bare, grey concrete. I stood there for a while, mouth agape, before I spoke.

'What are you doing?' I asked carefully, so as not to frighten her.

'Making a nursery,' she replied with the same nonchalance as if she had just said, 'Making a peanut butter sandwich.'

'Oh,' was all I could manage.

'I thought a nice yellow would do. We can sand back the picture rails so they'll match the floorboards. Of course, we'll have to sand those back too.'

'Mmm,' I said, slowly backing out of the room.

At that point I felt a migraine coming, so I poured myself a bourbon.

When the nesting urge comes, don't fight it. You'll only make things worse for yourself.

## EQUIPMENT

If you're a skier, you'll know that you need a lot of equipment to maintain your habit: skis, goggles, boots, stocks, gloves, roof-racks and, if you're a total wanker, a wardrobe of après-ski gear complete with fluffy boots. If you play a sport, you've probably got bags of outfits and various sporting trimmings like boots, shin-pads, sweat-bands, mouthguards and the obligatory tube of foul-smelling muscle ointment.

Parenting also requires a wide range of specialist baby gear. The first two basic items of equipment that you need are:

- a bigger car; and
- a bigger home.

And to get these, of course, you need a bigger income. Simple, huh?

Then once you've got your big car and big home, you will have lots of empty space to fill up with baby stuff. But be warned! A quick stroll through the local baby equipment store will leave your head spinning at the almost infinite number of products, gismos and accessories available on the market. And if you were to say to the nice shop assistant behind the counter, 'I'll have one of everything, please,' then you'd better have brought a fleet of removal trucks to transport all of your new acquisitions to your home – which would need to be the size of the town hall.

You have to be selective and wise in your stockpiling. I mean, when Adam and Eve had kids they didn't have all the gadgets and gismos that we have to have now, and they seem to have got along all right. So before you go off on a mortgage-busting spree, sit down with your wife and work out what you need and what you can afford.

If you're planning on having a few kids, it's probably more economical to buy. But if you don't want to outlay the cash up front, some items can be rented. Remember too that some things might be given to you as presents. If you're lucky enough, you may have friends who have just finished their own baby saga and are willing and ready to off-load some of their gear onto you. The classifieds also contain a wealth of second-hand goods. When buying second-hand, you should always ensure that an item has a tag stating that it conforms to Australian Standards. Be particularly vigilant for equipment which doesn't cut the mustard; you don't want your baby having anything to do with cheap, shonky or dangerous products. The Department of Consumer Affairs has brochures and web pages which provide copious amounts of detailed and valuable information.

Another thing. And this is an important one.

Avoid the trap of buying stuff simply because it suits your decor or because you're trying to live up to some sort of baby-magazine designer photo-spread ideal. I know a couple who bought one of those old-style English nanny prams because they thought they would look cute going for a walk in the park with it. The pram did look great ... but it didn't fold up, so they couldn't put it in their car, and it didn't store easily. It was also next-to-impossible to clean. In short, it was pretty bloody useless.

So, whatever you buy:

- Make sure it is strong.
- Make sure it is storable and will fit into your home somewhere.
- Make sure it doesn't fit into the baby's mouth.
- Make sure that after you buy it, you still have enough money for food for the rest of the week.
- Make sure it is washable – preferably capable of withstanding a hose-down in the backyard. Some products come certified with an International Radiation Symbol sticker. This means it has survived a nuclear explosion and, as such, has a good chance of making it through six months of use with a baby.

If you're still stuck not knowing what to buy, get your hands on a copy of the latest edition of *The Choice Guide to Baby Products* (Australian Consumer Association).

Below is a list of some other things you might find helpful.

# NURSERY

## Baby Zone

Your baby needs a place to live. Some parents like to have their baby room in with them. They like the security of knowing that the baby is nearby and feel that it provides more comfort and closeness for their baby rather than it being all alone in some dark quiet room somewhere. I know some people who have done this and found it to work very well. One couple I know, however, did it for a few weeks, but found it exhausting because they woke up every time the baby moved or made a noise.

I also know some parents who decided to have their baby not only in their own room, but in their bed. This worked well for them, although it's not something I'd personally advocate. I did fall asleep once with Rachael in our bed and I had the worst, most interrupted sleep of my life. General medical advice also tends not to promote this option because of the risk of the baby getting lost in the sheets and blankets, the risk of them falling out or sliding down and getting trapped between a wall and the bed and the risk of a heavy sleeper (or parent who has had a few drinks) rolling on them.[1]

Personally, I like my own space and believe it is a good idea for a baby to have their own space too. Preferably, this should be some place where you won't be disturbed by it too much – say, for example, Brazil.

For Rachael, we were fortunate in that we had a spare bedroom which we could convert into a nursery. If you are going to make a similar conversion, whatever you do, don't look at the pictures of nurseries in baby magazines. These have been designed by architects, outfitted by interior decorators and photographed by professionals in the homes of millionaires.

Real nurseries are small, cramped and smelly.

---

1. SIDS KIDS brochure endorsed by the Royal Australian College of Physicians

When Georgia came along, we didn't have another bedroom to convert into another nursery and it wasn't practical to put her in with Rachael. So we 'built' a bedroom in the hallway. (When she got older, she became room-mates with Rachael while Matilda took over the hallway spot.) No matter where your baby goes, there are a few bits and pieces that will make life a lot easier. A fan or heater help to control the extremes of temperature. A comfortable chair with a rug and footstool are nice for night-time feeds if feeding in bed is impractical.

Another necessity is one of those wind-up musical gismos designed for soothing babies off to sleep. Unfortunately, the only tune available on the market is Brahms's 'Lullaby'. You know the one. It goes, 'Da-da-daa, da-da-daa, da-da daa-daa-da-dah-dah. Brahms, of course, was a sadist, and you will soon discover that hearing this tune over and over and over and over is something akin to Chinese water torture.

## Sleeping Zone

New babies need a place to sleep. They should go into a bassinette, cradle or cot, something nice and cosy. Normal-sized beds are too big and down the track there's the risk of them rolling or crawling out of it. (As I said before, by all means share your bed with your baby. That is, if you don't mind sleeping on the knife-edge of the bed, being kicked in the ribs all night long, and having your chance of producing further offspring destroyed for several months.)

Be careful not to get sucked into baby-magazine fantasy advertising. A colonial-style cedar crib with decorative carvings and lace coverings may seem desirable, but it will cost you a fortune. And if you think the baby gives a stuff about the aesthetics of its crib, think again. I know of one family who put their baby in a sturdy washing basket. Now that's what I call ingenuity.

Because of the risk of SIDS, the baby's sleeping space should be free of bits 'n' pieces. These include loose bedclothes, quilts, doonas, pillows, fluffy toys, bumpers, water bottles and electric blankets.

Some cradles rock. These can be useful in swaying babies off to sleep, but you should make sure they don't swing like the pirate ship ride at your local amusement park. It is not good for babies to be upside down. It is recommended that a cradle does not swing more than 10 degrees from its standard position.

As your baby gets bigger, a cot will be more suitable for its nocturnal wrigglings. The cot must have tall sides so your baby won't fall or climb out of it. It must have a mattress that can withstand multiple rinsings in toxic bodily fluids. And if it has wheels, they should be lockable.

Don't be tempted to paint the cot. Your baby will soon grow razor-like teeth and they will spend a great deal of time gnawing away at the bars. And as we all know, paint is *not* one of the five major food groups.

## Clothing

Babies are much smaller than adults. As such, attempts to dress them in your own hand-me-downs will be an abysmal failure. They need singlets, booties, beanies and warm outfits. Jumpsuits, matinee jackets and nighties are ideal, depending on the weather. Most babies start off in a Size 000, which just shows you how small they really are – they don't even register on the scale!

As they get older, you will need to continually expand and upgrade their wardrobe at an almost bank-busting rate. It is sensible to buy for practical reasons, as opposed to making a fashion statement. But don't run off to the shops straight away. If you have a lot of friends or rellies, clothes tend to be a standard present for newborns. When Rachael was born, we had to use a shovel to move all the clothes she got as presents. In fact, she got so many that Georgia and Matilda were set for years of hand-me-downs.

*as opposed to making some fashion statement …*

However, I have discovered the one disadvantage to hand-me-downs. Now, when I flip through our family photo albums, I can't tell which of my kids is which because they're all dressed the same.

## Changing Zone

When changing or dressing babies there is a panoply of items that you need, including pins or 'snappies' (clips), nappies, pants, lotions, creams, wipes, plastic bags, liners, tissues, gasmasks, welding gloves and an industrial furnace to destroy any contaminants. It's best to establish a spot somewhere where all this paraphernalia can be centralised and contained.

You can always use the floor as a change-table, but this means getting up and down like a jack-in-the-box all day. If you have the space, you could invest in a free-standing change-table which has shelves for all the bits and pieces and a comfortable mat on top for the baby. If you buy one, make sure it is sturdy.

The main problem I found with change-tables is that they are designed for Hobbits. If you stand over six foot like me, that slight stoop will give you a back ache which will stay with you for the whole day. An alternative that worked very well for us was a simple foam mat that we sat on top of the baby's chest of drawers. This was high enough for me and it meant that we didn't need to clutter up the room with another piece of furniture.

A word of warning, though: new babies are pretty docile in that they haven't yet figured out how to wriggle, twist and claw their way away from you while you're trying to change or dress them. But as they get older, they develop a lemming-like ability to throw themselves off change-tables. Never leave a baby unattended on a change-table – not even for a second. Get all the stuff ready *before* you put the baby on the table. If you have to turn away to get something, keep one hand firmly planted on the baby.

## Baby monitor

If the nursery is a distance from your bedroom or main living area, you should get a baby monitor so you can switch it off when you hear the baby cry.

You especially need one if you have had the nursery sound-proofed, or if you've built it in your nuclear shelter, three storeys underground.

## Lighting

In the first weeks you will probably check on the baby quite a lot during the night. This is of course assuming that you can *see* the baby. To a sleeping baby, an ordinary ceiling light is like an aircraft coming in to land on its face. It is understandable that it will not be happy about this.

A simple, inexpensive night-light will solve the problem. These are very small, soft lights that are so low in intensity they don't even register on your electricity meter. They allow midnight checkings without midnight awakenings.

## Decorations

It's funny how the decor of your home changes once you have kids. Our place was once the domain of stylish black-and-white photographs and arty prints. Now the walls are covered in posters of rabbits wearing waistcoats, train carriages with stupid grins and gigantic bananas clad in stripey nightwear.

No wonder our kids have nightmares.

It's nice to decorate the nursery so that it is colourful and interesting. There are countless posters and friezes available that contain an enormous array of cute animals, numbers, letters and nursery-rhyme characters. Avoid the ones depicting vampires or naked women. Also avoid hand-painted imported Italian originals. These will wreck your bank account and won't look so good once mashed egg has been smeared all over them.

I hung a *Terminator 2* poster in the nursery while Meredith was in hospital. When she got home, she was very angry.

Don't do this.

Not even as a joke.

## Fluffy toys

There are many mysteries in our universe:

- Why is reality television so popular?
- Who shot JFK?
- What happened to Harold Holt?
- Why do Scouts say 'Dib dib dib'?
- What are the Colonel's eleven secret herbs and spices?

None of these are as perplexing, however, as the mystery of the fluffy toys.

We have over one hundred fluffy toys in our house. We didn't buy any of them. They were all gifts. We have fluffy bunnies, fluffy bears, fluffy ducks, fluffy cows, fluffy donkeys, fluffy monkeys, fluffy penguins, fluffy pigs, fluffy dogs, fluffy versions of every character from every ABC kids' show and Disney movie, and every kind of fluffy marsupial imaginable. Worse still, half of them squeak or contain jingly bells.

The scary thing is that we only started with about twenty. Pretty freaky, hey? So where did the others come from? Clearly they are breeding. They are planning the conquest of our house. One night we'll awake to hear muffled squeaks and jingles coming down our hallway and then it will turn into a B-grade horror film called *Night of the Fluffy Toys*.

Don't buy fluffy toys. They will get into your house anyway.

And one more thing. Keep fluffy toys out of the baby's bassinette or cot. It's fine to have them on a bookshelf or windowsill, but latest SIDS prevention advice is to keep them well away from sleeping spaces. Aside from restricting air flow, they are just scary as hell to a baby.

## HYGIENE

### Nappy Buckets

If you are going to use cloth nappies, you need a convenient place to soak the dirty ones. The World Health Organization advises against using your kitchen sink. And if you use your bathroom sink, shaving becomes unpleasant.

Buy two big buckets with lids and chuck the nappies in these. Store them in the bathroom or laundry – somewhere near a tap and where spillage won't matter. Make sure the baby can't get to them.

### Bath

Babies need to be cleaned. However, they're not very good at doing this themselves. Unlike us, they can't just hop under the shower. The best way to clean them is to give them a bath – but the one in your bathroom is like an Olympic swimming pool to them. You'll waste a lot of water on such a small person and also get a bad back from stooping all the time.

Your baby can either hop in the bath with you or, since

they're so small, you can bath them in a sink or the laundry tub. We didn't have a suitable sink, and our own bath was too big to be practical, so we bought a small plastic bath. These are readily available, inexpensive and can be put on a sturdy and safe kitchen or bathroom bench. To accompany the bath, you will also end up buying an expensive assortment of flannels, towels and squeaky toys all plastered with cute ducky motifs.

## Assorted Bits and Pieces

There are many little bits and pieces you will need to have with you when bathing or changing your baby. I'm not sure what they're all for, but since everyone else seems to have them in their baby's nurseries, you don't want to be seen to be negligent.

You need baby oil, olive oil, bath oil, engine oil, baby lotion, baby powder, a lambskin rug, an old stocking stuffed with oatmeal (don't ask), flannels, baby shampoo, zinc cream, a soft brush, cotton wool balls, cotton tips, tissues, methylated spirits, soft towels, a comb and several jars of unidentifiable lumpy grey stuff.

## FEEDING

### Bottles and Things

To feed a baby, you need:

- two milk-swollen breasts; or
- a tin or jar of milk formula with a bottle kit.

Later you'll need:

- a pantry full of powdered cereals, fruit gels, custards and purées;
- a collection of cute baby placemats, tablecloths, crockery and cutlery; and
- a highchair (see below).

Here's something I didn't know before we had children: breastmilk can be bottled too. This raises the question: how do you get it into the bottle in the first place? You use a breast pump, of course.

When I heard the words 'breast pump' for the first time, I had visions of Meredith entangled in the irrigation pump on my Uncle George's farm – a huge, greasy diesel beast which smokes and coughs noisily in the corner of his shed.

Fortunately, breast pumps aren't like this. They are small and dainty. You can get manual ones, which are like wide-mouthed syringes, or electric ones with a little motor. Once some milk has been 'expressed', it can be stored and labelled in plastic bags or ice-cube trays and frozen for later use. Your wife can build up a supply over a period of time. This is very useful for the babysitter if you and your wife go out. Of course, as with using formula, you need to buy an assortment of bottles, teats and a sterilising kit. When the baby gets older, the bottles can be used for water or juice.

## Bouncer

As our babies grew, we found a bouncer was a great way to get them off the floor and sitting semi-upright so they could have a look at what was going on in the world around them. Please note my use of the word 'floor' in the sentence above. Bouncers are only for use on the floor and should never, ever be put on a benchtop or table. Like the name suggests, they are just too likely to bounce off.

Being a history teacher, I noticed something very interesting about baby bouncers. They share exactly the same design and structure as medieval catapults, which were designed to hurl large and usually flaming objects through the air with the intent of causing much damage at the receiving end. It is very important, therefore, that you never depress and release the back of a bouncer too quickly – the results will be catastrophic.

## Highchair

About the time babies start sitting up by themselves they also start on more 'solid' foods. However, if you attempt to have them join you at the dinner table, you will find they disappear through the cracks in your dining-room furniture.

A highchair is therefore a good investment. The baby can join you for dinner at the table and all your dinner guests can get a good view when it dumps a plate of spaghetti on its head.

Make sure the highchair is cleanable (it will survive a dip in an aluminium smelter), strong (it won't collapse) and secure (it has a harness and your baby can't make like Houdini from it).

## TRANSPORT AND MOBILITY

Babies can't walk.

They don't even crawl for six or seven months, or even longer.

Even once they learn to crawl they are still pretty slow. Something as simple as going to the corner shop will take you hours – to say nothing of the damage done to the baby's knees. So modern baby-gear designers have come to the rescue by inventing many accessories for baby transport.

## Car Travel

It's hard to believe, but every once in a while, when I'm at a set of traffic lights, I will glance at the car next to me and see a parent bouncing a baby on their knee. Or even worse, with the baby tucked inside their own seatbelt.

Kids must be restrained in cars. Strapping them into adult seatbelts doesn't work (they just keel over) and simply invites police fines and disaster in the event of an accident. For example, if you are travelling at sixty kilometres per hour, with your baby unrestrained and you crash, the effect would be like dropping the baby from a second-storey window onto concrete. I'm sure no self-respecting parent would ever do that to their baby.

By law, you must have a capsule to transport your baby around in your car. This will be your baby's home in the car for a while (until the baby is either six months old, weighs nine kilograms or is longer than seventy centimetres). The inner chamber of the capsule detaches to make a convenient baby-carrier – convenient for short periods of time, anyway. If you don't want to buy a capsule, many baby goods stores and even some general hire places rent them.

When your baby gets a bit older it will graduate to the dizzy heights of a child seat (a moulded plastic seat complete with racing harness which is strapped to the car seat) and then finally a booster seat (a cloth-covered moulded foam seat which uses the car's seatbelt as a restraint). If you are buying a second-hand car seat, check that it hasn't been involved in an accident or is otherwise damaged. Check for vomit and other unsightly bodily fluid stains on the upholstery. If the harness is frayed, send it back to the manufacturer. Some manufacturers replace the straps free of charge.

If you drive an old-model car, check that it has a restraining bolt hole. You need this to secure both capsules and seats. When Rachael was born, we were driving an ancient van which didn't have a bolt hole, so we had to have a bar fitted across the back.

Don't wait until the day your baby is due to leave hospital to find out that your capsule won't go in your car! Go and have a look for that bolt hole right now. Well? Go on, then!

## Day-bag

Whenever you go out with a baby, you need to take a survival kit called a day-bag with you. We have one which we call 'The Tardis'. This is because it is bigger on the inside than it appears on the outside, and it holds more items than the laws of dimensional physics dictate should fit into it.

It contains everything a baby will ever need: sunscreen, nappies, plastic pants, snappies, hats, dummies, bottles, tissues, cotton tips, those wet-wipe things, spare clothing, books, soft toys, jars of slushy food, spoons, bibs, plastic bags, a lambskin rug, an orienteering compass, 40 metres of rope and a mobile phone with a speed dial to Police Rescue.

## Pram

Babies may be small, but they get heavy after a while. You can't simply carry them all the time. Being on wheels, a pram allows you to transport your baby around without having to bear too much weight yourself.

With our climate, it is important to find a pram that will provide shade for the baby. Some prams have extendable hoods or umbrella attachments, but you should at the very least be able to jerry-rig a towel on it to provide cover.

The pram we bought cost us more than my first car. It also had more features: eight rotating wheels, a reclining seat, four-way wheel-locks, independent steering, full reversibility, a luggage compartment, a shade-hood, a rain-hood, compression shocks, adjustable handles, a seatbelt, a running-board and *Ben Hur* chariot wheels which could easily shred the ankles of anyone stupid enough to get in our way. It could do thirty to forty clicks without getting speed-wobbles, it was light to push, comfortable for the baby, easy to clean, and we could fold it up without watching an instructional video. It also doubled as a cot on outings.

The newer style of jogger prams have become very popular in recent years. You have no doubt seen these, often as they whiz past you on the footpath in front of some health-nut parent in lycra. These three-wheel joggers are designed for more robust travel, as evidenced by the fact that they look like robotic all-terrain vehicles from Mars expeditions. They have large pneumatic tyres, springed suspension, padded passenger modules, alloy tubing, racing harnesses, coffee-cup holders at the back, rain hoods designed to withstand cyclones, and GPS satellite capability. They are made out of tough camping-style material and have bold and inspiring names like *Terrain*,

*Explorer*, *Pioneer* and *Adventurer*. Such vehicles are great if you want to take your baby for a walk through, say, Kakadu.

You will use your pram a lot. Get a good one.

## Backpack

There are some places where a pram is impractical, like the west face of Mount Kosciuszko. Also, if you take your baby to the supermarket, you will need one hand to get things off the shelves and one hand to push the trolley and one hand to carry the baby or push a pram. That makes three hands, which is a problem for most people.

So what do you do?

You can take the baby in its car capsule and place it in the trolley, although this will only leave you enough room to buy two tins of soup and a stick of celery. Fortunately, big supermarkets now have all sorts of fancy baby-friendly trolleys: those sporting reclined seats for newborns, more upright ones for infants, and even trolleys like golf buggies for twins. And then there's the good old pull-down basket on the regular shopping trolley. Of course, there are plenty of other places where there are no trolleys (most shops other than supermarkets, in fact), and this is where backpacks and slings

*slings are good*

come in quite handy. The front-slung snugly or sling is useful for little babies (just like the natives in *National Geographic*), while the backpack is more suitable for bigger ones.

At first I thought we could just stuff the baby down inside the backpack I'd taken around Europe. After all, it was very spacious, had a strong frame and many colourful cloth badges from places of interest that I had visited. Funnily enough, the baby didn't like it very much, and people in the street looked at me like I was some kind of weirdo. So we bought a baby backpack with good padding and straps. These are great for an outing to the zoo or shops or pool or even just for a walk to the park. Your baby sits up high behind you, allowing them to get a good view of the action and also show what they think of you by dribbling on your head and yanking huge handfuls of your hair.

Traditional baby slings have grown in popularity in recent years. These consist of a giant loop of cloth which sits on one shoulder and down across your chest and back. There's also a long, stretchy piece of fabric which you wrap around your body in a complicated way and then tuck the baby down inside it. These are popular, especially among residents of hippy communities, but if you have trouble tying anything more complex than a reef knot, then this is not for you. They allow for intimate contact with the baby (and for your wife, breastfeeding on the run) while keeping your two hands free for doing whatever it is your two hands want to be doing – washing, cleaning, vacuuming or abseiling.

## Baby Walker

Look, to be honest I'm not too impressed by these things and my advice to you is to steer well clear. They look cute in ads, but walkers give babies a mobility they may not be ready for – kind of like giving a ten-year-old the keys to your car. In a walker, a baby gains the capacity to travel around your house at approximately 30 kilometres an hour and use their vehicle as a battering ram. A walker also helps the baby to stand upright and reach expensive and forbidden domestic equipment.

I'm from the old school who believe that babies will walk when they're good and ready, and that it's a bit pretentious to push them. It also seems that babies put in walkers get used to the support they provide and are slow in becoming independent walkers anyway. Most importantly, I think walkers are just plain dangerous. Houses are too full of stairs and inclines and sharp corners and electric cords to accommodate aspiring Formula One drivers.

The Departments of Consumer Affairs and Fair Trading strongly advise against putting your baby in a walker.

## Playpen

As opposed to prams and backpacks and slings (which are all designed to enhance baby mobility), a playpen is designed to do exactly the opposite; namely, encourage baby *im*mobility.

When babies get a bit older they like to move around the house searching for things to destroy. It can be difficult to monitor their movements all day, so some parents put their babies in a portable jail called a playpen. This is an interesting piece of equipment because it's actually designed for the benefit of the frustrated parent, not the baby.

Some parents swear by their playpens, but I can't personally recommend them because the only time I tried to put Rachael in one she didn't enjoy the experience. She made me aware of this by taking off her nappy and creating some interesting new patterns on the carpet with the contents therein. I haven't tried since then.

If you want to get a playpen, use your common sense. Look for strength and stability. Watch out for splinters, toxic paint, sharp edges, finger-jamming hinges and head-squashing bars. Even then, don't assume that your baby's relative lack of mobility allows you to leave it unsupervised. Just think of our carpet.

So where exactly does all this leave you? With a house stacked to the creaking rafters with baby junk. And what exactly has all this cost you? To help you work out your overdraft, I have made a rough calculation of the cost of parenting three daughters during their first five years.

| | |
|---|---:|
| Lost income | $200 000 |
| Tarago (second-hand) | $30 000 |
| Extensions to house | $150 000 |
| Bedroom furniture | $3000 |
| Preschool | $5000 |
| Swimming lessons | $3000 |
| Ballet lessons | $1000 |
| Ballet shoes | $250 |
| All other shoes | $750 |
| Excess water bill | $800 |
| Food thrown onto floor | $1000 |
| Pram | $750 |
| Car seats/capsules | $350 |
| Nappies | $3000 |
| Indestructible cutlery and crockery | $50 |
| Carpet shampoo | $400 |
| Plumber (when nappy went down S-bend) | $650 |
| DVDs of 'The Wiggles'/'Bob the Builder' | $300 |
| Repairs to DVD player | $175 |
| Jewellery lost by inquisitive toddler | $6500 |
| Pony | $1200 |
| Food, stable, shoes, saddlery, worming drench for pony | $4000 |
| Classified ad in newspaper advertising pony for sale | $10.50 |
| Aspirin | $200 |
| Video camera | $1500 |
| Video camera tapes | $350 |

As you are starting to realise, raising children is not cheap. In fact, current research suggests it costs the average family approximately $450 000 to raise two children to the age of twenty.[2] Fortunately, I didn't know this figure when our kids were born, thereby saving me extensive doctor's bills for ulcers and blood-pressure medication.

It's pretty easy to look at that dollar figure and be put off. Don't be. Sure, having kids will reduce your disposable income for a large part of your life, but so what? It's worth it. What else are you going to spend your money on? Your train set? Nice clothes? A convertible? Beer? (Don't answer that.) Having kids is a good and worthwhile thing to spend your money on.

But before we leave the subject of shopping forever, let me give you a final word of advice. Watch out for 'feelers'. Feelers are total strangers who accost you at supermarkets and baby stores and social functions and, upon spotting your pregnant wife, descend *en masse* and rub their hands all over her swollen front bit as if she is public property. 'Having a baby?' they coo. 'Oohh, lovely, lovely. My, he's a big one. Is he going to kick? Are you going to kick, little baby? Goodness me, what a big kick!' And just like that, they're gone.

I'm glad that this behaviour is inflicted only upon pregnant women. I'm not sure I would like complete strangers putting their hands on my testicles and saying, 'Oohh, lover-ly, lover-ly!'

## GET AN EDUCATION!

In 1830, Sir Walter Scott wrote to a friend, 'All men who have turned out worth anything have had the chief hand in their own education.' This applies particularly to fatherhood. My perception is that most guys are like I was in my pre-father life; that is, they don't have the faintest idea about pregnancy, labour or caring for a baby. It is totally foreign to them. Completely out of their life experience.

2. Paper presented on behalf of Canberra University's National Centre for Social and Economic Modelling by Richard Percival and Ann Harding at the Australian Institute of Family Studies Conference, Melbourne, February 2003

But if you want to be an active and involved dad, you can't simply tag along for the ride, watching from the sidelines with a sense of vague detachment. You need to start asking important questions and finding out the facts. What happens during pregnancy? What happens during labour? How do you look after a child? Did I remember to put the bin out? What happens if I faint? And how exactly did my wife get pregnant in the first place?

In short, as Scott said, if you want to be of any worth as a father, you need to start educating yourself. Self-education will achieve three things. Firstly, it will help you understand what medical personnel are talking about. For example:

'Mr Downey, the episiotomy caused a caesarean epidural and I'm afraid your forceps were cervixed in the panic. As a consequence, our foetal monitor led to bonding with the cradle cap. Colostrum should do the trick, but if you're still concerned, go down to the pelvic floor and ask to speak to Braxton Hicks.'

Secondly, it will help you know what to expect; for instance, what happens when you go to the hospital and to what extent your life and bank balance will be ruined from now on.

Thirdly, it will help to fortify you against the visual spectacle of the birth itself.

Thomas Hopman was a boy in my Personal Development class at high school. I remember him because whenever we watched a film even remotely related to pregnancy or childbirth, his eyelids would start fluttering and eventually he would slump, keel over and hit the floor. This would inevitably drive the class into a rabid frenzy – perhaps the reason why we never got to see one of those films in its entirety. Perhaps this is the reason I was an ignoramus about fatherhood.

If you have delicate sensibilities, like Master Hopman, go to your local DVD library and search out their stock of childbirth and parenting documentaries. Borrow a DVD that has an explicit birth sequence in it. If it's in stereo, so much the better. Take it home, switch off all the lights and play it on your giant plasma television with the volume turned up full. Repeat this process until you can watch it without flinching. This will build up your resilience.

Aside from documentaries, there are a lot of regular films which have babies in them. (See Appendix 1.) Bear in mind, however, that most of these films are rubbish.

There are a number of other ways you can start learning. The very fact that you are reading these words is a sign that you have made a start (even though it is likely this book was given to you by your wife or mother ... ). Well done! However, no single book will give you all the answers, options, opinions and views on childbirth and parenting. My advice is to read – or at least browse through – as many books and magazines and websites as you can get your hands on. Libraries and second-hand bookshops are usually a reliable source. Practices and beliefs relating to pregnancy, childbirth and parenting can be quite different overseas and they also tend to change over time, so try to stick to the more recent Australian publications. Also, most newsagents have an entire shelf devoted to childbirth and parenting magazines. You can spot them because they have those soft-focus shots of mothers on the cover. And if you're a 'non-reader', go to the library and say you want a *Where Did I Come From?* book for your five-year-old son. These have lots of cartoons and are pretty easy to follow.

An important step in your education is to familiarise yourself with the place where your wife is going to have the baby. Hospitals usually run education evenings, which include tours of the labour and maternity wards. During these tours a midwife will run through the sequence of events likely to occur from the time you and your wife arrive at the hospital to the time mother and baby are happily recovering in the maternity ward and father is sleeping soundly on the chair in the corner. You are shown the place to report to, the waiting rooms, the delivery suite and the maternity rooms. You'll see all the high-tech equipment and the low-tech equipment and get to ask questions. You also get to find out where the really important things are, like the toilets, shop and cafeteria. It's also worth noting the location of the car park and drop-off places in case you are in a hurry.

On our first tour, one young guy pointed at a large silvery bucket at the base of a bed in the delivery suite. 'What's that for?' he queried.

There was a pause.

'Slops,' said the midwife dryly.

Several men were visibly shaken by this response. A deathly silence fell over the room. We moved on, but none of us were ever the same again.

Some hospitals have information nights, usually featuring a couple of speakers or presenters. If they're going to show films, though, don't eat before you go. Hospitals are also a good source for pamphlets and brochures covering a number of parenting issues and providing information on support organisations.

Many hospitals offer 'birth education classes' as well. For me, and my guess is that for many other guys, these classes are the primary source of information about, and preparation for, the birthing process. Our classes ran for five or six consecutive Tuesday nights and were great in educating Meredith and me on a whole range of things. We learnt about pregnancy and labour, listened to talks, watched videos, drew pictures, looked at a PowerPoint presentation and stuffed plastic babies through plastic pelvic bones. We did breathing exercises and panted at each other. We took off our shoes and learnt all about coping with contractions. We rolled around on the floor, screamed, slapped our thighs and swayed back and forth. We learnt about back massages and options for pain relief. I learnt about being a support person for Meredith. We asked questions and practised birthing positions. We leaned into beanbags, squatted down, crawled about on all fours and knelt. On the final night, one of the mums from the maternity ward came down and gave us a baby-bathing demonstration – with a real live baby and everything!

There is a certain sense of redundancy in doing some of these activities and exercises, because as a man, obviously you're not the one having the baby. However, it does help you to get into the mindset of childbirth and also break down any barriers of awkwardness or embarrassment you might be feeling about trying to support a woman who is screaming and thrashing and gnashing her teeth at you.

So get into it! Read books, surf the internet, watch DVDs and go to classes. It's the only way you'll learn.

## TO PLAN OR NOT TO PLAN?

In the 'old days', a pregnant woman had little say in what happened during her labour. She was merely there as a baby incubator, and the labour set-up was arranged for the convenience of the doctor. Supposedly, this is why many women gave birth in the Universal Television Position (UTP) – on their backs with their feet up in stirrups. It was nice and handy for the doctor. In reality, this is a lousy childbirth position because it doesn't allow the birth canal to open up fully. Also, the horse tends to get in the way. (Boom, boom.)

(I know a guy who had heard that women give birth in the position the baby was conceived in. He was concerned because he didn't want his wife giving birth while doing the Mexican starfish. But that's another story.)

The last twenty years have seen a growing resistance to the enforced compliance of the UTP. Women are now encouraged to be knowledgeable about the impending birth and to participate in the decision-making process. This is a good thing. But like most things, you can go too far.

A lot of couples work out a birth plan. They do a bit of reading, discuss the options available in the birth process and then custom-design their own 'ideal' birth. The plan might consist of a series of statements such as:

- *We want a painless birth.*
- *We don't want a caesarean.*
- *Forceps are not to be used.*
- *We want the labour to last only five minutes.*

The problem with an overly elaborate birth plan is that, unlike your nursery decor, you can't pick and choose to any great degree what is going to happen when the baby comes out. You can pick a birth as much as you can pick the weather on your wedding day. As such, many couples get disappointed – some bitterly – that the birth wasn't what they ordered.

Many things can happen in the delivery room, from a medical emergency to some advised intervention from your doctor. The labouring mother may have a change of mind about what constitutes the most comfortable birth position. If and when this happens, there's no point saying, 'Hang on a second – let's consult the plan!'

It is in fact more common to hear the woman scream, 'STUFF THE PLAN! I don't care what you do, just GET IT OUT OF ME!'

So how do you strike a balance between wanting a custom-designed birth where you decide everything, and having no say in the birth?

You should know your options and discuss these as a couple with your obstetrician. It is OK to have preferences and hopes beforehand, but you both must remain flexible. For example, while Meredith was not keen on the idea of having an epidural, I certainly would not have discouraged her if she grabbed me by the throat and screamed for one in the delivery room. As it turned out, she needed no pain relief for any of the three births. What a woman!

And if the doctor said to me, 'Mr Downey, I'm going to have to do a caesarean section,' I wouldn't have responded with, 'I'm sorry Doctor, but I'm afraid that's just not in our plan.'

Some things you might need to be flexible with on the spur of the moment are:

## INDUCTION OR AUGMENTATION

If labour is going too slowly, the staff may decide to 'induce' or 'augment' the process.

Induction is an artificial triggering of labour when it doesn't start naturally. This may be because there is a problem with either the mother or the baby, or, as was the case with us for Rachael, the baby is late. (She was two weeks overdue and we thought she was never going to come out!) Induction tends to be offered when a pregnancy goes into its forty-second week.

Augmentation is simply a booster to the process which has already started naturally but is moving a little too slowly. Either way, this is an artificial means of telling the body to 'hurry up!' It can be done chemically, through an oxytocin or Syntocinon drip, or by introducing prostaglandin gel to the cervix. ('Mr Prostaglandin, this is Mrs Cervix. I'm sure you'll get along just fine.') It can also be done manually by rupturing the membrane inside the uterus with a long hook. This uncomfortable but speedy procedure is called an amniotomy.

But if you prefer an *au naturel* method, a brisk walk or a good swim can often get the wheels moving. I have even heard that a good bowl of vindaloo will kick things along, although I suspect we are heading into old wives' tale territory, and besides, does a pregnant woman really want the gastrointestinal side effects that invariably come with such a dish? Stimulation of the nipples is another tried and true method. (Her nipples that is, not yours.) I don't know if it actually helped Meredith, but I sure enjoyed it.

Sex is also said to be a good way of triggering the labour. Sex with a nine-months' pregnant woman is interesting, to say the least, but hopefully for her it's more fun than having a drip or an injection.

## PAIN-RELIEF OPTIONS

If the pain of childbirth is too much to bear, there are options available to bring relief. You can have a swig of bourbon or try to sneak a hit of laughing gas or simply shut your eyes, stick your fingers in your ears and think of a happy place. But while such methods may help *you* cope with the pain of childbirth, they won't be of much use to your wife, who, having a large baby pass through a small opening, needs it more than you.

Labouring women use many options and techniques to help them power through the childbirth experience and surf the pain wave. Many women report that a proactive approach and lots of preparation and exercise help them to feel in control during the birth. Many say how facing up to the pain (rather than pretending it won't be there) helps them feel determined, resilient and confident about what lies ahead, rather than being some sad victim.

Various breathing techniques and vocalising (sound and movement exercises like thigh slapping, fist clenching, chanting, rocking, etc.) that will assist women to manage the pain may be practised during birth classes. Yoga can also be helpful in preparing the muscles of a woman's body for the demands of birth.

Birth classes will also look at various birthing positions because – as mentioned previously – the on-the-back-with-feet-in-stirrups position is great for TV but terrible for childbirth. Ultimately, a labouring woman will find her own position of most comfort. For many, it is on all fours, in a bean bag, a semi-crouch or even reclining in water. An upright squatting position allows the woman the freedom to move to accommodate the movements of the baby as it emerges from her body.

The mind is the most powerful tool in dealing with pain and so visualising is also encouraged. Instead of thinking about the pain the pain the pain, the woman focuses on the outcome and purpose of the pain, namely the baby. She visualises dilation and the baby emerging through the birth canal or other happy thoughts like pinning you against a wall and punching your head in because you're the bastard who got her here in the first place.

You can also help her cope with the pain by massaging her, applying hot packs, setting up relaxing music and talking to her. But even with all these options, sometimes the pain is too much and the labouring woman wants drugs to help her cope. You can generally tell this is the case when she puts her hands around your throat and screams, 'PAIN RELIEF – NOW!'

About 90 per cent of women in Australia use some form of pain-relief drug during birth.[3] Women in country areas tend to use less, with the highest users being women in Sydney private hospitals.

In terms of pain relief, most modern hospitals no longer stock hip flasks of whisky or bullets to bite on. Anaesthetics in Australian hospitals have come a long way since then. One option is a TENS machine, much like the one your physio uses on you when you stuff up your back playing a sport you are too old to play. Another option is a combination of nitrous oxide and oxygen – laughing gas – just like the stuff you get at the dentist. It supposedly dulls the pain and makes it feel like someone else is experiencing it in the next room. While the gas is very safe for both mother and baby (because it is quickly expelled from the body), it doesn't really do much for some women. However, it does work well for others. If you're quick, you might be able to get a few lungfuls yourself.

A pethidine injection is a stronger form of pain relief; this is an opiate which relaxes the mother and alters her perception of the pain. It is not usually used in the later stages of the labour because it may affect the baby's breathing. Some women don't like the pethidine option because it can make them drowsy and nauseous and they lose some sensation and don't fully 'experience' the birth – which is ironic, because this is exactly why other women like it.

---

3. According to NSW Mothers and Babies 2003 Report

The big-league option is an epidural block. This is when a local anaesthetic is injected via a catheter into the woman's spinal column, which knocks the lower half of her body unconscious. She doesn't feel a thing but remains awake to witness the event, which is probably like watching someone else give birth (even though her angle of vision will be quite unique!). Once again, some women don't like epidurals for this very reason. It also restricts movement and the woman's ability to push, which could in turn prolong the labour.

It is important that you read up on the pros and cons of pain-relief options and discuss them with your doctor prior to the labour.

## BREECH BIRTH

Most babies are born head-first. This is so they can see where they're going on the way out.

Don't be alarmed, however, if your baby has a crack down the middle of its featureless face. It's probably a breech baby, which means it has no sense of direction and is coming out bum-first. Breech babies can be born normally, but if difficulties arise, an episiotomy or caesarean might be necessary.

## EPISIOTOMY

This is where the doctor deliberately cuts your wife's vaginal opening to make it bigger and easier for the baby to pass through. The idea is that making a small, specific incision prevents large and uncontrolled tearing.

Yes, tearing. As in ripping. I am talking about torn skin and muscle. Whether torn, ripped or cut (makes your head spin, doesn't it? Just another reason I'm glad to be a bloke), stitches are applied afterwards to help in the healing process. And when I use the word stitches, I'm not talking about little teensy paper-cut-on-the-finger stitches. I'm talking about *stitches* stitches. *Big-time* stitches. Meredith has a friend who had fifty-two of them. Yes, you read it right. If you re-read that last sentence, it will still say … FIFTY-TWO. I had a mate who almost amputated his leg in a skiing accident and *he* didn't have fifty-two stitches.

## CAESAREAN BIRTH

This is where the baby is removed surgically. It used to involve a vertical cut from the mother's throat down to her knee, but advanced medical technology means that a modern caesarean is only a small horizontal cut along her bikini line. The cut may look small, but because it involves cutting through abdominal muscles, the mother can't do anything too strenuous for several weeks afterwards. In fact, a full recovery from a caesarean takes about a year.

A birth like this will usually take place if there are complications with the baby – such as it being in a weird position – or with the size of the woman's pelvis, or sometimes if she's having twins. Usually the decision to perform a caesarean is made well before she even makes it to the hospital. (Take, for example, the case of American woman Kristina House who is listed by Guinness World Records as having had eleven children delivered by caesarean section!)

Sometimes the operation needs to be done on the spur of the moment. The doctor will suddenly yell, 'We gotta go C-section – NOW!' Everybody in the delivery suite will start running around shouting 'STAT! STAT!' and the doctor will jerk a thumb towards the door and say, 'Get him outta here.' Three burly hospital aides will drag you out while you scream your wife's name, and choirs and violins will begin to filter through the hospital's PA system.

Anyway, that's what happens on TV.

Just a few decades ago, Australia had a caesarean birth rate of just 5 per cent, well below the World Health Organization estimate of 15 per cent for any given population. However, the rate of caesarean births in Australia has now jumped to 20 per cent, with this figure doubling again for older mothers. This increase has been attributed to such factors as the recent increase in medical litigation cases (causing doctors to opt for more intervention) as well as the popularity given to elective caesarean births by celebrity mothers. Some women also see it as a way of shortcutting around the pain and getting straight to the baby bit, while others are concerned about potential damage to their pelvic floor.

The rising popularity of caesarean births is a concern to many in the childbirth profession. They see it as negation of the fact that the woman's body is designed to give birth. It is a natural process, not something foreign that has been inflicted upon her, like a disease to be avoided. Then again, those kinds of words are easy for me to write. I'm a guy and don't have to face up to the whole thing myself.

My mother had a complicated pregnancy and as a result, I was a caesarean baby. That's why I have a big head and have trouble finding hats that fit me.

## BABY-REMOVING DEVICES

Sometimes, in the middle of a delivery, the baby gets cold feet and decides not to come out. Or like a caver who's had one too many doughnuts, it can get stuck in the claustrophobic confines of the birth canal.

To help it get out, there are two main baby-removing devices:

- *Forceps*, also known as Gigantic Baby-Grabbing Pliers. These are used to grab the baby's head and pull it out (the whole baby that is, not just the head). They may be used if the baby is stuck, or if exhaustion or the anaesthetic have rendered the mother's pushing ineffective.
- Some hospitals use a piece of equipment called a *ventouse* to get a good grip on the baby's skull. Think of it basically as a vacuum cleaner with a toilet plunger

attachment on the end. You will be pleased to know that this is purpose built and there is little risk of your baby being sucked inside out.

Both of these options may cause some markings or bruising on your baby's head. Don't be alarmed – the bruises go away.

## INCUBATOR OR HUMIDICRIB

Most babies have a 'normal birth' and adjust to the outside world very quickly. Some, however, can have complications and need to be monitored closely. This can be the case with premature babies, low birth-weight babies, babies with severe jaundice, babies with breathing irregularities, and some caesarean babies.

If your baby comes into one of these categories it might be placed in a sealed crib, or incubator, which is hooked up to lots of machines that go 'beep' and 'ping'. These machines help to monitor your baby's bodily functions, including body temperature, breathing, and possibly feeding as well. Many parents feel intimidated by all the tubes and gauges and flashing lights. They may also find the incubator frustrating because they are physically separated from their baby by a plastic shield. But you can still touch your baby through portholes, and spend time sitting next to it and talking to it. Often normal feeding is possible as well.

Ask the staff questions about your baby and the incubator. The staff in special care nurseries are used to anxious parents and will help you to feel more comfortable about the situation. In any case, remember that your baby won't be in there forever.

## WHAT'S IN A NAME?

It is a truth universally acknowledged that the single biggest cause of marital disputes in Western society arises over the choice of names for an impending child. Actually, finding a name that *you* like is pretty hard. Finding a name that you and your wife *both* like is next to impossible. Because it takes a lot of time and many nights perusing any one of thousands of 'names for babies' books and websites, you should pick possible names for both sexes well before the child is born. This gives you both plenty of time to fight about it.

Some parents don't put too much thought into the names they pick for their children. Some even choose on a whim. The problem here, of course, is that the kid is stuck with the name for life. This is a particular problem during the school years, because we all know that *children can be so cruel.*

So here are a few helpful hints. DO NOT choose any names from the following categories:

- *'One-off' names belonging to an incredibly famous person or character:*
  Frodo, Elvis, Azaria, Elle, Madonna, Tarzan, Hamlet, Cher, Noddy, Voldemort, Bono, Sting, Goofy, Santa, Indiana, Tupac, Homer, Oprah, The Artist Formerly known as Prince, Darth, or any person from the Bible, such as Jesus, Noah, Moses, Samson, Delilah, Maher-Shalal-Hash-Baz, etc;
- *Bad persons of history:*
  Idi, Judas, Adolf, Benito, Lucifer, Attila, Imelda, Ghengis, Lucretia, Saddam, Osama;
- *Anything sounding vaguely American:*
  Chet, Chip, Chad, Chuck, Hank, Mack, Bud, Pierce, Duke, Randy, Dubbya;
- *Anything sounding vaguely English:*
  Winston, Winthrop, Bayfield, Beauchamp, Sebastian, Culthorp, Lester, Your Majesty;
- *Stupid Hollywood inanimate-object names:*
  River, Skye, Storm, Leaf, Axl (sic), Shade, Thorn, Park, Summer, Moon Unit, Jet, Stone, Rock, Branch, Cotton, Wankel Rotary Engine;

- *Double-barrelled names:*
  Peggy-Sue, Ellie-May, Billy-Ray, Sally-Jesse, Lee-Harvey, John-F, Loretta-Lynn, Sylvester-Anne;
- *Impossible-to-spell names:*
  Siobhan (pronounced Shuv-orn), Ymobhij (pronounced Jer-e-my);
- *'Blonde, big-breasted and brainless' names:*
  Dolly, Cindi, Barbi, Lucy, Trixie, Dixie, Pixie;
- *Library-monitor names:*
  Myron, Herman, Vernon, Sheldon, Donald, Nigel;
- *Names that imply sexual ambiguity:*
  Boys: Percy, Cyril, Cecil, Julian;
  Girls: Butch, Spike, Gay, Les;
- *Checkout-chick names:*
  Gladys, Cheryl, Beryl, Doreen, Maureen, Kayleen, Darlene, Raylene, Charlene, Carlene, Ethel, Sheila, Laverne, Shirl;

*bad persons of history ...*

- *Names for twins:*
  William and Benjamin (who will be known for the rest of their lives as The Flowerpot Men); Jack and Jill; Abbott and Costello; Ernie and Bert; Mickey and Minnie; Patience and Prudence; Rocky and Bullwinkle; Barnum and Bailey; Best and Less; Sodom and Gomorrah; Porgy and Bess; Itchy and Scratchy; Simon and Schuster;
- *Names for higher multiples:*
  Tom, Dick and Harry; Curly, Larry and Moe; Ginger, Fred and Jack the exploding axolotl; John, Paul, George and Ringo; Julian, Dick, Anne, George and Timmy the Dog; Harpo, Zeppo, Groucho, Chico and Karl; Bobby, Peter, Greg, Marcia, Jan and Cindy; Gilligan, The Skipper, Mr and Mrs Howell, Ginger, The Professor and Mary-Anne;
- *Names that are innocent enough by themselves but make a lethal combination when mixed with particular surnames:*
  John Thomas, Dwayne Pipe, Wayne Kerr, Phil McCavity, Hugo First, Mary Christmas and, of course, that evergreen favourite, Richard Head. (My own family – the Downeys – have shown a great lack of thought in this regard. Just ask my Uncle Sid or Aunty Ida.)
- *The least popular names of all time (according to D. Wallechinsky, et al.'s The Book of Lists 2):*
  Boys: Altair, Faber, Aubrey, Stockton, Florian, Lyman; Girls: Rosemede, Hilary, Myra, Vaughan, Shobhana;
- *Any names that appear in songs:*
  Roxanne, Sharona, Lola, Fernando, Dolly, Ziggy, G-l-o-r-i-a, Eleanor Rigby, Jake the Peg.

Of course, if you follow my advice, your kids will be called Karen, Kathy, Jane, David, John or Michael, which is a little dull really. But you shouldn't follow my advice anyway, because as you may have guessed I am a complete hypocrite with one daughter called Georgia (as in 'on my mind') and another called Matilda (as in . . . well, it's obvious isn't it?). But it's not my fault. They were Meredith's choices.

Another problem, which I will just throw in here for the heck of it, is that even when you *do* agree on a name, as soon as the baby is born you will look at it and realise that the name is wrong.

'He just doesn't look like an Irving,' you will say.

Then you have to start all over again.

## TO CUT OR NOT TO CUT?

One thing that you really should discuss before the child is born is circumcision. In short, should you circumcise your child?

This is a real source of contention and the cause of the ruination of many of our dinner parties, as proponents of one view or the other express their opinion in a most narrow-minded, forceful and socially inappropriate manner. Well, I've got no particular drum to bang, but for what it's worth, here's my view. You can take it or leave it.

If it's a girl, no. (Duh!)

If it's a boy, no.

*But I was circumcised, damn it, and it didn't do me any harm,* I hear you cry. *Why shouldn't I have my boy 'done'?*

According to my wife, it's because circumcision is cruel, unnecessary and has no medical justification.

I have less noble reasons.

When I was born, circumcision was standard practice and as such I received the cruellest cut as a matter of medical course. It was 'the done thing'. I was quite happy about this, because twelve years later I 'looked the same' as all the other naked boys in my high-school PE change-room. To have a different organ in this situation meant suffering the worst taunts.

Now that it's the twenty-first century, however, the scissors have been put away and foreskins across the land are breathing easy. It is now no longer 'the done thing'. The Royal Australasian College of Physicians does not view circumcision as a routine procedure and these days only 10 to 20 per cent of Australian boys get circumcised. The point is that twelve years from now, all the boys in the high-school PE change-room will be uncut and the poor kid *sans foreskin* will be the odd one out, not to mention the butt of all those jokes about doctors who make hand-luggage out of foreskins they've collected. Don't subject your son to that.

If you really are obsessive about it, you should probably talk to your doctor – but be warned, if you're going to try to convince him or her to circumcise your newborn son, you'd better have a good argument.

## TO JAB OR NOT TO JAB?

Sometimes on talk-back radio you'll hear some debate about immunisation, with both camps offering passionate arguments for and against. This is probably something you should also discuss with your wife and doctor before the birth of your child. (Immunisation, that is, not talk-back radio.)

Let me be honest with you. Although I have a St John's Ambulance Certificate, I do not consider myself to be in any way knowledgeable about medicine or the ethics of vaccination. Having said that, I think immunisation is a good idea – a view, I might add, which is held widely by the medical profession and the World Health Organization. I have no desire to risk my kids getting polio, bacterial meningitis, whooping cough, measles, mumps, tetanus, rubella, diphtheria, bubonic plague, halitosis or dyslexia.

The majority of kids in Australia are immunised. It takes place at regular intervals, largely when your baby is between two and eighteen months of age, with a few top-ups in adolescence.

It's important that you don't get swayed by emotional arguments, forceful opinions or even go along just because that's what everyone else does but rather look at the hard data relating to the risks and benefits of immunisation. It's probably best for you to consult your doctor or paediatrician for details.

## WHEN YOU LEAST EXPECT IT

It's getting towards that time ... the due date. All your preparations are now complete. Family and friends are fully primed and on alert. The nursery is fully furnished and ready for operation. You've been to classes. You've picked the names. You've read the books. You know the drill. Your wife's bag is packed and sitting by the front door. Your mobile phone is fully charged and programmed with important phone numbers (parents, parents-in-law, friends, pizza delivery). The cameras are loaded. The car is fuelled and pointed in the direction of the hospital. All you need now is for the baby to come out.

Babies come out when they want to.

The problem here is that you can't spend the final months following your wife around on the off-chance that the contractions will start. When Meredith was in her final weeks with Rachael, I must admit to being something of a concerned, some would even say obsessive-paranoid, father-to-be. Whenever I was out, I phoned every couple of hours just in case Meredith had gone into labour in the lounge room and needed me there straight away.

I remember coming home from work one day during her 'final week'.

The house was empty.

Meredith had been rushed by ambulance to the hospital, where she was giving birth at that very moment!

I panicked and phoned the hospital. 'My wife's pregnant and her name's Meredith and she's not home. She's having a baby and I just got home and my name's Peter and she's not here and she's due this week. Is she in the labour ward? Is it a boy or a girl?'

Even as the words tumbled out, I realised how pathetic I sounded. The nurse did her professional best not to sound too patronising or annoyed, but I could tell she thought I was an idiot.

'She's not here. She's probably shopping. Goodbye,' was all she said.

She was right. Meredith was shopping and I was an idiot.

Make sure you've got your phone with you at all times, or that at least someone knows where you are and how to get in touch with you. Then, the only thing left to do is wait for the bat-signal.

Because when that happens ... it's time to party.

# CHAPTER FOUR

# SURVIVING THE HOSPITAL

*'When you do actually go to the hospital, DON'T wear
good shoes. They'll only get ruined.'*

## A BRIEF HISTORY OF LABOUR

It is certainly true to say that the labour process itself has
changed over the course of history.

In her classic *Clan of the Cave Bear* stories, Jean M. Auel tells
about life at the dawn of time. When the pregnant woman felt
her first contraction, she was exiled to a dark corner of the cave
with a few woman friends to writhe through the agony of
childbirth on a mastodon-skin rug. Meanwhile, the 'mate' and
future father sat with the men of the tribe around the fire to
discuss the day's hunt. The men knew instinctively that labour
was a 'woman thing' and that this was not to interrupt their
evening men-of-the-tribe chat around the fire. Many hours later,

after all the action, the newborn would be presented to Dad, who would grunt, scratch himself a few times, and pass the kid back.

He definitely was not a modern man.

Well, times may have changed but it's funny how some things never do. The dark and smelly cave has been replaced by a bright and smelly hospital. The ochre paintings of bison on the cave wall have been replaced by pastels of flower arrangements in the waiting room. But up until just recently, the inherent sexism of the labour process had pretty much remained with us.

Not too long ago, men were still nowhere to be seen near a birth. You're probably familiar with the television sitcom stereotype of labour. I was brought up on this and was almost disappointed when I discovered that it wasn't like this anymore. You know the stereotype I mean: four or five dads-to-be, eyes bleary from hours of coffee, anxiously pacing the waiting room floor, eagerly expecting the door to open and the nurse to stick in her grinning head and announce, 'Mr Downey, it's a (insert appropriately) boy/girl/not sure yet!' I would then receive pats on the back while handing cigars out to all my paternal comrades.

*not a 'sensitive new age man' ...*

It doesn't sound too different from the cave, does it? Fortunately, times have changed sufficiently that we dads now have quite an important role to play in the labour process. No longer do we have to wait by the fire in the cave. No longer do we have to wait in the waiting room. *Now* we get to participate. We are there. Point-blank. Living colour. Surround-sound. The whole bit. And this is lucky for us, because being present at and participating in the birth of your child is a really wonderful experience.

Terrifying, yes. But wonderful.

In fact, now we've gone to the other extreme and there is an increasing trend for not only fathers to be present at the birth, but the rest of the family as well! Some sources have reported that about a third of couples having children in birth centres or at home elected to have their other kids present at the birth. Personally, I can think of nothing more likely to cause long-term psychological damage in a child, but I suppose everybody is entitled to their opinion. Hey, why not also invite your parents, brothers, sisters, cousins, uncles, aunts, gym instructor, neighbours, workmates and football team to come along? Make a day of it! Get your friends to 'bring a plate'!

But remember, you are not there just to spectate. And (heaven help us) you are certainly not there to be a cameraman capturing everything on your digital camera (see below). Your presence at the birth is primarily for one purpose and one purpose only: you are there to support your wife. You are there to soothe her, to encourage her, to reassure her. To do this, you must be totally focused on her needs and on the labour process.

## SHOULD I BE AT THE BIRTH?

Yes.

## BUT, WHAT'S IT LIKE?

Before we go further, I want to make one point clear. The point is this. Childbirth is PAINFUL. It may well be a natural and normal part of a woman's biological journey, but it is still painful. Very, *very* painful.

God was not kidding when He said, 'With pain you will give birth to children.' (Apparently there *are* women – in the minority, to be sure – who genuinely don't feel any pain with childbirth, or who feel only mild discomfort. And there are even women who have described it as physical pleasure! But I've never met one of them.)

There is nothing in a man's natural span of life that even comes close to the searing agony which accompanies a baby tearing itself from its mother and being squeezed out into the world. Sure, there are kidney stones and industrial accidents involving heavy machinery and testicles, but there is nothing that lies almost inevitably in a man's biological routine.

Unfortunately, we have fallen victim to pathetically unrealistic television portrayals of labour. These try to convince us that labour involves little more effort than an afternoon aerobics session. The hapless woman pants a few times, blows a few breaths through clenched teeth and then, with a Herculean push and a final gasp, gives birth to the baby. The woman has merely shed a light sweat.

This is crap. Total and utter crap.

Childbirth is actually like trying to push a camel through the eye of a needle.

The camel is very big.

The needle is very small.

The needle will experience a lot of pain.

A while ago a friend of mine lent me a cassette – one of those motivational things by some American business guru. There is one phenomenal part of the tape where the guru says, in a thick mid-Western drawl, 'With thuh burth of mah furst chahld, my wahf and ah had uh paaynless layburr.'

I played this to Meredith. She didn't think it was very funny.

I'm sure it was painless ... *for him*. Although I'm not a medical giant, I am now a veteran of three births and therefore think it's fairly safe for me to claim that, generally speaking, childbirth is not really very physically painful for us men. That is, unless you're a Cayapo Indian male. They have ropes attached to their testicles for their labouring partners to yank upon during contractions, just so *they* know what it feels like. But I digress.

This next story may help you arrive at some understanding of the pain of childbirth. Soon after I found out that Meredith and I were going to be parents, I naturally became quite inquisitive and anxious about the whole labour process. But aside from textbooks, I had no source of information. Then one day at an afternoon tea we met an old friend who had just had a baby herself.

What a perfect opportunity! Unashamedly, and in retrospect idiotically, I opened our conversation by asking her if childbirth was 'painful'. The look on her face betrayed the fact that she clearly knew I was the most stupid man on earth. Fixing me in her steely stare, she said:

'Imagine you are holding an umbrella.'

*Mmmm, OK so far*, I thought.

'Now,' she said, pausing for dramatic effect, 'insert it into your penis.'

At this, my legs involuntarily crossed and my eyes began to water. I tried to break eye contact, but she could see that her words were cutting me like a knife. She held me in her gaze and pushed on mercilessly.

'Now open the umbrella,' she hissed.

With alarm bells clanging loudly in my head, I staggered to my feet in a feeble attempt to escape the anguish in my groin. But there was no escape. She grabbed my arm and snarled in my ear, 'Now pull it out. Yank it – hard.'

She was revelling in the paralysing effect of her words. And her words had had the desired effect.

'That's what childbirth is like,' she snickered as I hobbled off.

# LIGHTS ... CAMERA ... ACTION!

A few years ago I spent a bit of time teaching English in Japan. At one point I had some time off so I did what any self-respecting tourist would do: I packed my backpack and hit the road in search of adventure and major scenic attractions.

One day I ended up in the Todaiji Temple staring at the 1200-year-old, 450-tonne Daibutsu, which is the largest bronze statue on Earth. I remember this not because of its breathtaking size, nor because of its artistic lines, nor for the overpowering sense of history that the place commanded. I remember this place clearly because of the busload of American tourists who arrived just as I got there. These people had obviously been briefed on 'American Etiquette Overseas' and had all had lessons in How To Be a Typical Texan Tourist in Foreign Climes. They had twangy accents. They had gaudy clothes. They had big hats. They had condescending attitudes ('The Giant Buddha in Dallas is twice as big as this, Cyndi'). But most of all, they had cameras.

Lots of cameras.

Lots and *lots* of cameras.

Super 8. VHS. 35 mm. Automatic. Disposable. SLR. Panoramic. Box Brownie. You name it, they had it.

Now, most people would go to a tourist spot, have a stickybeak around for a while and then snap off a few shots to remind them of the place in years to come. Not these guys. They were clicking, whirring and reloading before their golf shoes had even hit the gravel. Within seconds they had deployed ranks of tripods and were grinning and posing for their automatic timers.

The ironic thing was that some of them were so busy taking photographs that they never even bothered to look at the statue itself. They didn't take time to enjoy the experience of being there, but instead were only concerned about having a souvenir for later. I particularly remember one tobacco-chewing gentleman, who obviously had a penchant for doughnuts, walking up to his wife – who was having a look around – and saying, 'Snap it now, Martha. We can look at it later.'

I swear it's true.

The reason I've indulged in this somewhat tedious anecdote is as a tenuous segue into my next point.

The birth of your first child is a fairly momentous occasion and as such you may feel the need to capture it for posterity. Fair enough. But how far are you going to go with this camera thing? How many photos are you going to take? How long are you going to video for? And more importantly, *what* are you going to shoot?

There are four main rules that you should adhere to when shooting film during childbirth.

## RULE ONE: DISCUSS IT WITH YOUR WIFE BEFOREHAND

This is perhaps the most important rule of all. During labour, your wife will be in no state to direct the photography. So discuss beforehand what she wants or permits you to photograph. Anecdotal evidence suggests that most people want just a few tasteful snapshots taken after the baby is cleaned and wrapped up. I have heard of some women who want no cameras of any description within 50 metres of the delivery room. I have heard of others who want every single gory detail captured at point-blank range on both video and still camera.

If the latter is the case with you, and you take thirty-six close-ups of wife with legs akimbo and baby coming out, whatever you do, DON'T take the film to one of those photo-labs in a busy shopping centre where the developed films scroll out of the machine in the shopfront window. If you do, a small crowd will gather, usually made up of your wife's boss, your ex-girlfriend and the minister from your church.

If you use your phone to take some jpegs or mpegs, resist the temptation to broadcast them to your family and friends in some kind of pseudo real-time coverage of the birth event. While you might be quite moved by the whole experience, your colleagues probably don't want to receive footage of 'placenta being delivered' while they're having their lunch.

## RULE TWO: DISCUSS IT WITH YOUR OBSTETRICIAN BEFOREHAND

As a courtesy, you should raise the question of photography and videography with your obstetrician and ask about their attitudes in different potential situations. It is likely that they will not have any objections at all about you taking still photographs. However, you cannot assume that a hospital or obstetrician will allow unrestricted videotaping. In the US, and in some Australian hospitals, an anxiety about litigation has caused the introduction of restrictions, or even bans, on filming. This is especially so in the case of a caesarean birth (either planned or emergency), or during a birth where unexpected complications arise.

Your obstetrician may want to retain the right to ask you to stop filming. In the case of the caesarean, there are issues relating to the sterility of the operating theatre as well as the necessity for permission to be sought from all of the medical team involved in the operation. There are also more practical issues to consider, like you simply getting in the way (see Rule Four) or the obvious problems posed by the possibility of you fainting at the sight of your wife being cut open with a scalpel.

## RULE THREE: REMEMBER YOUR ROLE

Keep in mind that you are by your wife's side during the birth to provide support. Don't be fooling around with your cameras when your wife needs words of assurance or simply your company and attention. You're not going to be much use to anyone perched in a corner scrolling through your memory card looking for bad photos to delete from your last holiday.

In addition, you certainly don't want to antagonise her with unreasonable photographic requests.

Don't, for example, say things like:

- 'Hey, that was great – can you pull that face again?'
- 'Can you lift your legs just a *bit* higher?'
- 'Don't push, don't push, I've got to reload!' or
- 'Hey, Doc, get outta the way, will ya?'

Which leads us to:

## RULE FOUR: DON'T GET IN THE WAY

If you want to take lots of photos, using a flash may be a problem. The doctors, nurses and especially your wife (and, when it's born, the baby) don't want to be blinded by constant explosions of light. It may be wise, therefore, to use a low-light film or adjust your digital settings so your photography can be unobtrusive.

If you want to shoot video during the birth, that's your business, but stay out of the way. Medical personnel may not mind if you set a camera rolling in the corner, but you can expect

*the need to capture it for posterity ...*

opposition if you bring in a three-camera rig with light stands, mixing console, dolly grip and gaffer.

## ZERO HOUR

The phone rings.

OK, this is it. Zero hour.

The final grain of sand has fallen through the nine-month hourglass and it is time for the baby to come out into the real world. This may be signalled by *a show*, which is a euphemism for the expulsion of a big, bloody, messy glob of mucus which has been plugging up your wife's plumbing for the past nine months. It may also be signalled when *the waters break*. This is where the uterine cocoon ruptures and all the amniotic fluid spills out like a scene from *The Dam Busters*. (Great fun if you're at a restaurant!) Or it may be signalled by the commencement of regular *contractions*, which is another euphemism for the pain caused by your wife's uterine muscles getting together to dilate and thin the cervix in preparation for pushing the baby out. This is the beginning of the first stage of labour.

For some reason, I always assumed that my wife's contractions would kick in at about 2 am, several days before the predicted date. I imagined scrambling for the car keys in pyjamas and slippers and making a dash to the hospital in the freezing dead of night. Of course, contractions can come at any time, and the onset of contractions certainly does not mean that the baby is about to be born within minutes. Some people find that labour can be a very lengthy, and consequently exhausting and frustrating, process.

This frustration can be even worse if your wife has a false labour. The contractions kick in, everybody gets psyched up and you go to the hospital, but after a while it becomes apparent that nothing is going to happen, and the nurses send you home. Your wife's body was playing a practical joke on her! These premature contractions are called *Braxton Hicks' contractions* and are the uterus's way of practising for the strong contractions needed during labour. (I don't know what he did, but for his name to be applied to these false starts, Mr Hicks must have been a real bastard!)

It is also frustrating when the baby is late. Statistics indicate, in fact, that most first-time mothers will have their babies on average a few days after the due date. It is hard not to subconsciously psych yourself up for the due date, and you may be anxious if you only have a narrow window of absence from work. But then the big day passes. The next day passes too. And the next. And the next after that. And then after that the next day passes. Finally the day after arrives and then unceremoniously passes as well. The expectation and tension increases until you're a nervous wreck. It's like *Groundhog Day*. Every day seems exactly like the last. Basically, you just have to grin and bear it. *Que sera, sera ...*

We were pretty lucky with the births of our kids. For our first child, Rachael, I woke up on a Friday morning ready to go to work after a good night's sleep and was confronted by my wife saying, 'OK, I think this is it.' It was a beautiful summer's day. The sun was shining through the window and the birds were singing as we had breakfast. Rachael was born just after 11 am. She was two weeks late.

For our second child, we were just clearing the table after a very pleasant dinner when once again Meredith said, 'OK, I think this is it.' Georgia was born close to midnight. She was one day late.

For the third birth, I was sure we could get it right on the day – just to confuse our obstetrician. But then we travelled down the familiar road of one day, two days, three days late. Then on the fourth day, right in the middle of 'The Simpsons', Meredith said with great certainty, 'This is it.' Matilda was born a few hours later – twenty minutes off being an April Fool. Phew.

The point is that 'it' can come anywhere, anytime. It could be midnight or midday. You might be in bed or on a train or at a dinner party or driving a plough. (As a matter of fact, it could be now.) But when the time comes, there's no point saying, 'Can you just hang on a minute?' You must be ready. The bomb is about to go off.

There is one important thing to remember at this point. In the immortal words of *The Hitchhiker's Guide to the Galaxy*, **DON'T PANIC**. If it is not an emergency situation (i.e. the baby's head is sticking out), remain calm and in control. Do not, for example, run around screaming, 'What do we do?! What do we do?!' Do not run for the car semi-naked from your interrupted shower with shampoo in your eyes.

This is where all your careful planning pays off. If you are having a home-birth, start running the bath. Boil some water and tear up a sheet into strips. (I'm not sure why, but that's what they always did in 'Little House on the Prairie'.)

If you are going to the birth centre or hospital, give them a phone call. They'll probably ask you a few questions about the space between the contractions and their duration, and tell you when they think you should come in.

Most people make it to the hospital on time, but some don't. They might get stuck in traffic, their car might break down, or the birth may strike sooner than anyone could have predicted. If it is an emergency situation, again, **DON'T PANIC**. Remember, childbirth is a *natural and normal* thing. It has been going on ever since Eve said to Adam, 'OK, I think this is it.' Three hundred babies are born every minute in the world, most without the luxury of freeways and hospitals, so you're certainly not doing anything new. A woman's body is designed for childbirth. It is a fully automated process.

Nevertheless, there is a certain protocol to observe if you're not going to make it to the hospital. (Statistically, this is highly unlikely, but it does happen from time to time.) If you're in the car, pull over somewhere safe. Don't stop in the middle of an intersection or outside a boys' high school during their lunch break. If you're in a taxi, make sure the driver turns the meter off. If you can, get someone to call an ambulance.

Then do your support stuff, just like normal. Don't freak out. Your wife will need you more than ever before, and your panicking won't make things any easier for her. Help her to find her best birthing position, then get down near the baby-chute and catch it as it comes. Let the goop come out of its mouth. Wrap the baby up in a jumper or towel to keep it warm. Don't pull on the umbilical cord or cut it; the placenta will come out by itself. Then go directly to the hospital. Do not collect two hundred dollars.

The next thing to do is to place a classified ad in the paper offering your car for sale for about 20 per cent of its market value.

One final word of advice: if and when you do actually go to the hospital, DON'T wear good shoes. They'll only get ruined.

## STAGE ONE: BEFORE BIRTH

Birthing is something which still retains a certain sense of mystique in our society. Some people liked being born so much that they go to 'rebirthing clinics' to try to experience the whole thing all over again. Some states even have a public holiday to commemorate the wonder of the birthing process. This is called Labour Day.

As you can see, my knowledge regarding birth is extensive but not very technical. So as you read this next section, let me remind you that although I am a doctor, my Doctorate is in education, not medicine. I am one of those guys you see on TV where, on a plane flight over the Pacific, a flight attendant asks, 'Is there a doctor on board?' and he puts his hand up and is bundled up to the back of the plane to deliver a baby despite trying to explain the mistake but they can't hear him over the woman's screams, and it's only after he's conducted a caesarean with nothing but plastic airline cutlery and a sewing kit that the confusion is explained among tears of joy. In short, don't rely on a word I say. Also, in any discussion of childbirth it is necessary to talk in generalisations because every pregnancy and every birth is unique. For example, take the following cases from D. Wallechinsky, et al.'s *The Book of Lists 2*:

- Georgias of Epirus was born in his mother's coffin during her funeral.
- In 1970, Grete Bardaum gave birth to twins – one black and one white.
- In 1955, the Schee twins were born forty-eight days apart.
- In 1875, a seventeen-year-old girl became pregnant after a bullet fired in the nearby Battle of Raymond lodged into her uterine wall. She didn't know that the bullet had already carried off part of a soldier's left testicle. Nine months later she gave birth to an eight-pound boy who had to be operated on to have the bullet removed. The soldier and the girl later married.

Hmmmm. Believe it . . . or not.

Trying to cover every eventuality of birth would be impossible, but here's a general overview.

OK. You've driven to the hospital and screeched to a smoking halt in the car park, waking an entire wing of patients who were just getting off to sleep. Suddenly you realise you've left your wife at home.

Go back and get her.

Drive back to the maternity wing. Grab someone wearing a uniform and tell them who you are and that you've arrived to have a baby. (Make sure it's a medical-looking uniform and that they are not a cleaner or caterer.) You will have already filled out forms and things a while ago, and as you've probably already phoned, they'll be expecting you anyway. Eventually you will be shown to a labour ward or delivery suite where the hard part begins – the wait.

Your wife may have a quick labour: You arrive at the hospital. The baby is born. The End.

Or your wife may have a long labour: You arrive at the hospital. You hang around for ages getting tired, impatient and hungry. The baby is born. The End.

In reality, it is common for the first stage of labour to be anywhere from two to ten hours long. During this time the contractions build in intensity. They get stronger, closer together and longer in duration. By the time of birth, the uterus has grown to be the biggest and strongest muscle in your wife's body, so you can imagine the strain this puts on her as the contractions increase.

Meanwhile, you are waiting for the cervix – the passageway out of the uterus – to get bigger; to 'dilate' until it is big enough for the baby to pass through. Some people refer to this process as 'waiting for the cervix to ripen', which, in my mind, always conjures up awful images of rotten fruit. But that's another story.

Normally the cervix is about 2 millimetres long, but it needs to thin and open up to about 10 centimetres to allow for the baby's head. If my crude mathematics serve me correctly, this expansion is an increase of several thousand per cent. To fully appreciate this muscular feat, contemplate the fact that the hole at the end of your penis is also probably about 2 millimetres. Pretty scary, huh?

From time to time a nurse will come along and give your wife an internal examination to inspect the degree of dilation and check the progress of the baby. After the first cervix inspection the nurse will probably say, 'Two centimetres', which is code for, 'You'd be lucky to give birth to a walnut right now.'

Fifteen minutes later, when your wife has experienced so much pain that she is sure you could drive a bendy-bus through her cervix, the nurse will come back, inspect, and say, 'Three centimetres.' The nurse will then go and phone your obstetrician and tell him how many more rounds of golf he could probably fit in before he needs to get to the hospital.

It is sometimes the practice at this stage for your wife to be given an intravenous drip. This may be glucose, which maintains fluid and blood sugar levels, or a synthetic hormone such as Syntocinon, which helps ripen (*cringe!*) the cervix. When Georgia was born, I asked the nurse for a bourbon drip but she didn't think I was very funny. She must have had a long shift.

So, labour can be long, painful, tiring and frustrating for mothers, many of whom by this stage are starting to have second thoughts about their babies and just want to go home and forget it ever happened. Once you see your wife going through contractions you will agree that there is no doubt the female of the species really drew the short straw as far as childbirth is concerned. However, you should also be prepared for the effects labour will have on *you*. Sure, you're not the one with the contractions, but you can't just stand back unaffected in the shadows either.

Childbirth for fathers is *draining*. It can be mentally taxing to focus on your wife for hours on end. It is also physically demanding. You might have a sore back and be on your feet the whole time, and you might not have eaten or had anything to drink for ages. It may be particularly difficult if your wife has laboured through the night and you've both been awake for over twenty-four hours straight.

Because it's probably the first time you've witnessed childbirth, it can also be plain *scary*. You'll be in a strange and perhaps sterile place full of machines that look like they belong in a submarine movie. Medical personnel will come and go and sometimes talk about things you might not understand. You might not be really sure that everything is going as it should for your wife, and on top of that, you may be anxious that the baby will be OK.

The experience can also be *harrowing*. The woman you love will be in pain. She will look at you with either pleading or accusative eyes and, aside from the aforementioned massages and assistance, there'll be very little you can do about it. It won't be pleasant watching her struggle through it.

On the positive side, however, childbirth is a *thrilling* experience. It is awesome to see your child come into the world. It can be very emotional to finally meet the fruit of your loins and realise, 'I'M A DAD!!!!'

As your wife nears the second stage of labour – the actual birth – you may notice her becoming vague. There will be a blank expression on her face and her comments will become more monosyllabic. Her breathing will change. All this is because a naturally produced opiate, endorphin, has entered her bloodstream. In short, she is stoned. She will internalise her thoughts, getting further away from the real world. Her body, meanwhile, will be racked by pain as the contractions get stronger and her cervix opens wider.

Throughout this entire process, remember that *you are there to help*. Don't let your mind wander – focus. Encourage and support your wife. Hold her hand. Rub her back. Hum her a tune. Talk to her. Reassure her. Wipe her face with a flannel. Stroke her hair. Help her move around. Help her maintain a comfortable position. If she is in the bath, pour water over her back. Let her get you in a head lock. In short, do whatever she wants if it will make her feel better.

Of course, this is assuming that you can actually *understand* what she is saying in the first place. Women in labour have a special, secret language which is largely incomprehensible to the male ear. For example, she may point at the ceiling and say, 'Grumph ... hoooo ... hoooo. Shup ... den ... plissss', which you will interpret as, 'Nice shade of peach on the ceiling there, isn't it?'

Later you'll find out that she wanted a foot massage and a grilled cheese sandwich.

When she was having Matilda, Meredith slowly twisted her arm up and pointed behind her back. She muttered, 'Harumph ... sheejh ... carrrmooon. Hhooo ... hhrruuufffff.'

I took this to mean, 'Give me a really hard back rub, just ... here', which I did. Later I found out she actually meant, 'Whatever you do, don't touch my back here.'

Just do your best.

Another thing you can do to help is encourage her to use the breathing techniques and exercises you practised in your birth-education classes. Breathe with her and coach her through the contractions. Remain calm and controlled. Be relaxing. Say positive things like:

- *That's it ... good ... b-r-e-a-t-h-e d-e-e-p ... You're doing great.*
- *Almost over now.*
- *Relax, relax, relax.*
- *Open, open, open, baby, baby, baby.*
- *I can see the baby's head.*
- *Oh Toto, I want to go back to Kansas.*

Avoid saying negative things like:

- *Wow, look at all that blood!*
- *Boy! I'm glad I'm not you right now!*
- *Hey, is that supposed to happen?*
- *Don't pull that face – you look silly.*
- *I don't think this baby's ever going to be born!*
- *Can you be a bit more quiet? You're embarrassing me.*
- *Did you turn the stove off?*
- *STOP BEING SO TENSE!*

Once upon a time, women were supposed to be quiet and dainty while giving birth. But this is an unfair request, if you think about it. Try this exercise:

- Put your hand on a solid surface.
- Hit it with a sledgehammer.
- Stand still and make no noise.

I bet you can't do it, assuming you're not one of these psychopathic villains in action films who hold their hand over a blow torch without flinching to show how tough they are. Of course you can't do it! If you've ever actually hit yourself like that, you know you scream, moan, swear, yell, pace back and forth, jump up and down, and so on.

'Noise and action' is a popular childbirth pastime. Encourage your wife to make whatever noises she feels like and to move however she wants to if it will help her cope. This could be rocking back and forth, slapping her hands on her legs, moaning, repeating words, pulling faces, breathing strongly and steadily, and panting. The main thing is, don't stand back snapping off photos of her behaving strangely. Join in with her.

As the second stage of labour approaches, the urge to push may become irresistible for your wife. Things at this stage can get a bit wild. Normally sedate women may scream abuse and say things to their husbands they'll later say they didn't really mean, like, 'I hate you for doing this to me', 'I never want to see you again', 'You're not really the father', and 'Let's have another baby straight away'. It is common at this stage for women's heads to spin 360 degrees while vomiting green bile all over the delivery suite.

## STAGE TWO: BIRTH

This is the stage during which the baby is actually born. It can last from a few minutes to a few hours.

Now, let us for a moment consider how the baby feels about being born. For the past nine months it has been happily floating in its own little world that it has come to call home. It spends its days sucking its thumb, dreaming, and practising for its black-belt exam. It probably really likes it in there and, if it had its way, would not come out until it was eighteen years old, thereby avoiding the terror of school and many awkward moments during adolescence.

Then all of a sudden, things turn sour. The nice warm fluid drains out and the baby is inexorably pushed downward towards an impossibly small hole as though it has been caught in some sort of vaginal tractor-beam.

As you can imagine, it might not be happy about this turn of events.

For this reason the obstetrician may decide to keep an eye on the state of the baby on its journey. This is done with a foetal heart monitor. A small electrode or sensor is placed on the baby's scalp and your wife's abdomen, and a machine making 'ping, ping' noises will monitor the contractions and let everyone know whether the baby is 'in distress' or not. If your wife has had an epidural she will almost definitely be wired for sound, because she won't be able to feel the contractions herself.

Meanwhile, the baby's head will be slowly negotiating the cervix and making its way through the pelvis. The crown of the head may now be visible. If there is a problem with the size of the passageway, an episiotomy may be performed.

At this stage, after much 'labour' from your wife, the head of the baby will pop out and turn around. There may be a short

*Ta-daaaaaaaaaa!*

pause, then with the next contraction the shoulders will be delivered, and finally the rest of its body. It will shoot out into the world in a flurry of blood, mucus and litres of unidentifiable technicolour fluids.

Ta-daaaaaaaaaa!

So, you're a dad!

Take a few breaths.

Snap off a couple of tasteful shots.

Look at the face of your child. Cuddle your wife.

Savour the moment.

If you want to cry, do it. You wouldn't be the first.

One day you'll look back and laugh.

## STAGE THREE: AFTER THE BIRTH

Straight after it's been born, the baby's throat may need to be cleared of all the fluid and mucus and guff that it's been soaking in over the past months. This is done by one of the nurses or the doctor by inserting a tube into the baby's throat and sucking it all out – an activity, I might add, that certainly does not appeal to me. The baby's reflexes will kick in and it will take its first breath. It will then be put straight away onto Mum's stomach for some warmth and a bit of a cuddle.

At first you may be surprised by how your baby looks. It might not be what you expected. This is because in commercials, on TV and in films, all 'newborn' babies are in fact photogenic eight-month-olds who have just had their hair shampooed. Most have had acting lessons, too.

Real newborns aren't like this at all. They are wrinkly little things covered in mucky, tomatoey gook. They are also coated in a thick creamy covering, called *vernix*, that looks like French onion dip. They are usually squashed and have weird-shaped heads, and they may have bruises or marks from the tight squeeze, or from a forceps or ventouse extraction. Some are born with jaundice, which makes them all yellow, and some are born with a fine covering of body hair, called *lanugo*, which makes them look like werewolves under a full moon.

In short, newborn babies are ugly and messy. All of my kids looked like Yoda when they were born. (But they're beautiful now. Really.)

Another shocking and little-discussed feature of newborns is ... well, how can I put this nicely? Um ... you see ... they have REALLY BIG GENITALS. Newborn boys are surprisingly well-endowed, and girls' parts can be quite swollen. Both boys and girls can secrete milk from their breasts. But before you get too proud of the fact that your newborn son looks like some super-human sex-god, his scrotum, which currently reaches to his knees, will get small again after a while.

If you look carefully you will also notice that your baby is still attached to your wife by a long, thick strand of grey spiral pasta. This is the umbilical cord. But your baby can't stay dangling out of Mum forever. (This would make even simple things like going to the cinema a virtual impossibility.) So the cord has to be cut. Some people ascribe great symbolism and significance to this event, and often the father is asked to perform the complex operation, which involves the highly technical process of squeezing a pair of scissors. Once the cord is cut, it is then sealed off with a clip.

If you do cut the cord, make sure of the spot, otherwise you might damage your son irreparably and – you guessed it – cause him much embarrassment in his high-school change-room twelve years from now. With Rachael, at first I thought that I had cut in the wrong spot, because her new belly-button was four inches long! But it's supposed to be like that. In the next few weeks the cord will dry out and drop off. If you're lucky, you will find the shrivelled remnant in the cradle. You can then have it bronzed and take it to work to show your friends.

Next, the afterbirth must be delivered. No, not in the same way that pizza is delivered. The afterbirth is all the stuff that comes out after the baby. It is like a giant peeled tomato, a red pillowcase that has been your baby's primary life-support cocoon for the past months. It is made up of the amniotic sac, the placenta and the cord itself. After the baby is born, the placenta will break away from the uterus and come out the same way. Sometimes an injection is used to encourage it along. When it arrives, the placenta will be inspected to see whether it is whole, or whether in detaching itself it has torn, leaving remnants inside your wife. If you're lucky, the doctor will shove it in your face and show you interesting things about it. At this stage, your wife might have to have some stitches if tearing has occurred, or if she has had an episiotomy.

Anyway, enough of this eye-watering stuff. If you are so inclined and if you ask nicely, the hospital staff might let you take the afterbirth home with you. It sounds weird, but some people really do it. I know a couple who went to their friends' place for a morning tea. It was a nice morning, with tea and cakes and pleasant company. Then the hosts, who had recently become parents, whipped out a shovel and a suspicious-looking plastic bag and invited everybody down to the backyard for an afterbirth-planting ceremony. Pretty gross if you ask me. Then again, it's better than being a cat. They eat their afterbirth, but at least they have the decency not to invite their friends around to watch.

*an afterbirth-planting ceremony ...*

# IN THE SILENCE

When the afterbirth has been delivered, most of the show is over. Equipment will be wheeled away. Some of the staff disappear. The mess is cleaned up. A strange quiet will fall over the room. The newborn is placed on Mum's chest for its first breastfeed so she can have a cuddle and her first good look at the baby she has been carrying around for nine months but hasn't yet met face to face.

Your baby will be given an Apgar score, which rates its skin colour, breathing, reflexes, heart-rate and muscle tone. The baby may also undergo a quick and simple hearing test. It will be weighed, cleaned up and possibly even bathed. The diameter of its head will also be measured. A hospital tag will be attached to its wrist detailing name, weight and time of birth. This is to avoid confusion and prevent parents from fighting over whose baby is whose later on.

For the first few days, the baby will receive a super-powered drink from its mother's breasts. This is called colostrum. As it can sometimes have a golden hue, it is often thought of as 'liquid gold'. It is thicker and stickier than more mature milk which will kick in a few days later. Colostrum is an amazing cocktail, more powerful and potent than anything that could be dreamed up in a chemistry lab.

Colostrum is a turbo charge for the baby, a concentrated power drink which does several things. It has a laxative effect, to give the baby's new digestive system the kick-off it needs. It has a nourishing effect, as it is chock-full of goodness in the form of, among other things, amino acids, minerals, sodium, potassium, vitamin A and E and caretonoids – whatever they are. And importantly, it has an effect on the baby's immune system. Colostrum is full of immunoglobins and so it acts as a kind of anti-virus booster and protector against the nasties in its new environment outside the protective confines of the womb. If colostrum could be refined and packaged and sold as a supplement, it is so potent it would probably be illegal.

At some point your wife might have the opportunity to take a quick shower, but she'll probably need your assistance.

And that's about it.

The baby will be put in a nightie and wrapped up tightly in a blanket. Then the staff will probably leave the three of you alone to get to know each other.

After the noise, pain and turmoil of the birth, it's really nice just to relax and enjoy your first moments alone together in the silence. After nine months of waiting, there is a certain sense of awe and wonder in seeing your baby for the first time. You will notice little things, like its fingers and toes, eyes and ears, and the folds of its skin. This whole experience can cause an adrenalin rush which will leave you on full power for the next three sleepless days.

And as the three of you sit there exhausted in the delivery room, you will start to think, 'Phew, it's all over.'

Don't kid yourself. Now the hard work really begins.

## BONDING

You have probably heard of this thing called 'bonding'. My *Macquarie Dictionary* defines bonding as something that unites individual people. It binds, fastens and holds together. This word is thrown around quite a lot in birthing circles. It refers to the process by which you feel joined to your baby; when you feel that 'it' is part of your family; when you feel an emotional involvement; a link that unites you both.

I expected this bonding to occur the moment the baby popped out into the world. I expected to look at it and experience a warm glow of love and attachment.

I didn't.

I expected it to be magical, mystical and instantaneous.

It wasn't.

When my kids were born, it was pretty amazing and all that. But I didn't feel 'bonded'. I wanted to. And I was wondering where the violins and soft focus were. Meredith, on the other hand, bonded straight away. As soon as the baby was in her arms and feeding, she was off with the pixies. She was stroking skin and looking at her baby with a deep look of contentment, love and adoration.

To be honest, it took me quite a long time to bond to my children. Sure I felt a little flutter when I held my own child for the first time or when a little hand squeezed my finger. But I wasn't as ga-ga as I had expected.

Looking back, I can remember several different points when I actually felt the bonding process occurring. These were times when the baby responded to me. The first time her eyes followed me. The first time she smiled or laughed at me. The first time she reached for me. The first time she fell asleep on me. The first time she vomited on me. The first time she said 'Daddaddadda' – at least, that's what I think she said.

In retrospect, I realise my expectations were as limited as expecting to love Meredith the first moment I saw her. Bonding is a relationship thing, and any social-theory textbook will tell you that a rich relationship or even a feeling of attachment doesn't occur at the snap of the fingers. It takes time.

Like most experiences in becoming a dad, everybody is different. I know of some guys who really did bond instantaneously. They picked up their newborn (yuck!) and almost swooned. The coming days were spent totally obsessed with this new addition to their family. These are the guys who have the six rolls of photos developed one hour after the birth. Stay away from them.

I know others who, like me, were fairly nonchalant at first towards their newborns, but warmed up after a few weeks.

Don't be stressed about bonding. It will come in its own time.

## CELEBRATING

Well, congratulations. You can now officially call yourself 'A Dad'. Welcome to the world of fatherhood.

Such a monumental step as this is cause for a monumental celebration.

As a child of the TV generation, I was always entranced by the depiction of proud dads celebrating the birth of their first child with their friends. This largely involved drinking champagne, making a lot of noise and, most importantly, smoking cigars. And come rain, hail or shine, I knew that this was what I was going to do when my first child was born.

And so Rachael arrived. I was so charged up after the birth that I didn't sleep for a few days. Everything fell into a kind of timeless euphoric haze which had started off with a great celebration party. I invited everybody I knew around to our place to watch gripping selections from the hours of video I had shot. Everyone congratulated me on the great job I had done. What an achievement! I could be proud of myself! That night, the el-champagno did flow and my pals and me went through a box of cigars. This is amusing in an odd sort of way, because the only thing that I detest more than champagne is smoke. But this was what had been programmed into my mind by years of sitcoms, so champagne and cigars it would be!

While I was celebrating and being thoroughly self-indulgent, my wife was lying exhausted in a hospital bed, trying to cope with the demands of a new baby. When I came down and hit 'the wall', not only did I feel physically exhausted and lousy, I also felt guilty that I had let her down like that. Perhaps I would have been better saving my strength and spending a bit more time at the hospital? Perhaps I should have postponed my celebration until both my wife and our baby could also attend? After all, they were the stars of the show who did all the hard work.

I had learnt my lesson. When Georgia was born, the celebrations were a lot more controlled. I only smoked half a box of cigars and only stayed up for forty-eight hours. And when Matilda was born I finally got it right. I celebrated with a small light beer and a pencil-thin filtered cigar. Then I went to bed early ... and lay awake all night.

# TAKE IT EASY

It is very easy to get excited about the birth of your first child. Even if you haven't quite bonded in a personal way, there is still a great sense of occasion and you are still riding the momentum of nine months of expectation. You feel like you have jetlag and time loses its meaning. After all, it *is* a pretty big deal, and usually all your friends make a huge fuss. And after witnessing the miracle of birth, it's little wonder you get emotionally carried away with the whole thing.

However, you can start to lose your perspective and begin to think that the birth of your child is the single most momentous event of the century. This is called *paternal tunnel vision* or, as the doctors call it, PTV.

The first signs of this syndrome are excessive photographing or videoing. Because everything is so new, and being such an important event, you want to capture as much as possible on film. For example, I snapped off a roll of twenty-four just of Rachael's feet. Fortunately, two of the shots were in focus.

The main problem, as any parent with two or more children will tell you, is that the first child ends up with fifteen photo albums, a box of three-hour video cassettes, their own webpage and a homemade DVD, complete with soppy soundtrack, documenting their first week of life. The second child ends up with one photo album, a video cassette and a few jpegs dumped on a CD. The third child ends up with some photos still in the packet (located somewhere in a suitcase under the house) and some video footage, half of which you taped over when you took your camera to a grand final.

Another symptom of PTV is an inability to talk about any subject other than your baby. You should take care to avoid lengthy monologues with neighbours, friends, relatives or colleagues regarding fatherhood. Remember that while your life has been turned upside-down, their lives have gone on as normal. Most will want to know how the birth went and how mother and baby are doing, but they don't want a sixty-minute re-enactment of the birth.

Many people find it quick and convenient to spread the good news to large groups of friends and family by sending an email. It's more time-efficient than contacting everyone individually, although the flip side is that it is less personal. But keep it simple. People want to know the baby's name and weight, how Mum is doing and how things went in brief. They want to see a jpeg or two of the new arrival. They don't want a 3000-word birth journal accompanied by gigabytes of jpegs and mpegs.

If you go to the pub for a beer with your workmates, you will find that they too probably won't want to discuss the ethics of intervention in birthing; they won't care about torn perineums; they won't want to debate the advantages of breastfeeding over bottle feeding; and they won't be interested in updates on the progress of baby faeces consistency.

There is also common decency to consider. Some things are supposed to be kept private. For example, I'm not sure your wife would appreciate you narrating graphic descriptions of her torn vagina or cracked nipples. I know my wife didn't.

I also made the mistake of subjecting our friends to video footage of 'us having breakfast on the morning of the birth', 'a quick tour of the maternity wing and miscellaneous interviews with interesting people I met there', 'mother and baby minutes after birth', 'floral arrangements in the labour room', 'me filming myself and free-associating in the car park after the birth', and so on. It was OK for the first two hours, but things turned sour after that.

None of my friends come to visit anymore.

## SHE'S GOT THE BLUES

I had heard about this thing called *the blues*, the period of moody sadness suffered by some women following the birth of their babies. But I knew instinctively that it wouldn't happen to my wife. 'The blues' were for other women; women who were emotionally weak or prone to depression in the first place. My wife, on the other hand, is just about the most level-headed, down-to-earth and fully-in-control person you are likely to meet. So 'the blues' didn't apply to her, right?

Wrong. During the last weeks of pregnancy and particularly during the labour itself, women overdose on their naturally produced opiate, endorphin. After the birth, most women have enough hormones pumping through their veins to knock down an enraged bull elephant at twenty paces. But then the opiate dries up and they go cold-turkey. Add to this the fact that childbirth is painful and physically demanding – women do not recover overnight, particularly if their labour was traumatic or if they had to have stitches. The whole situation is then aggravated by the fact that new mothers are tired from balancing altered sleep patterns (read: 'lack of sleep' patterns) and a continuous stream of visitors. There is also the nervous anxiety and mental pressure of being responsible for a new and fairly demanding human being. The result is a potent emotional cocktail known as 'the blues'.

Depending on your source, somewhere between 60 and 85 per cent of women experience 'the baby blues', which can last up to a couple of weeks. This is why, when you visit a maternity ward, somewhere in the distance you can always hear the twang of a steel guitar, the wail of a harmonica and a chorus of mournful female voices singing:

*I had a baby the other day*
*And I can hardly walk*
*My nipples are dry and cracked real bad*
*And my husband and I don't talk*
*I got the blues*
*I said I got those moody bloo-oo-ues*
*I got the baby-makin' breastfeedin' down 'n' out*
*maternity blues.*

All women will react differently, but the blues can be triggered off by almost anything and usually manifest themselves in mood swings and spontaneous crying. You can't argue with it or talk your wife out of it. Your job is to help and support her in the most appropriate way possible. Be sensitive and understanding. Encourage her. Comfort her. Talk to her. Hug her. Be there for her and the baby as much as possible. She needs rest, so help out by taking the baby or by managing the onslaught of visitors (see below).

Don't tell her what a great time you're having at home by yourself. Don't tell her about all the great parties you've been going to. Don't tell her she's being silly and that she should grow up and stop crying like a little girl.

Put your arms around her, damn it!

For some women, however, the blues don't go away. They just get worse. This is a serious condition known as *postnatal depression*. Sufferers can feel lost and confused, tired and miserable. The whole routine of domestic life with a baby can dull their senses. They may have trouble bonding with the baby. They may also feel emotionally on-edge and as though they are isolated from real life. Their world seems to be permanently off-balance.

Postnatal depression can last for months and sometimes even years. Be open to discussing this with your wife. Support her and spend time with her. Provide her with adult conversation. Tell her not to feel guilty or ashamed of her emotions. Help to organise the domestic routines and provide stability and order around the home. If appropriate, arrange friends or relatives to visit her. Find out about local groups which she can become involved in, such as mothers' groups, playgroups, Bible studies, and so on. Don't be afraid to seek professional counselling. Call your hospital or local baby-health or early-childhood centre for more information.

Whatever you do, don't ignore it or pretend it will go away.

Your wife needs you, damn it!

## GUESTS

It's good to have friends. Of course, your friends and relatives will want to share with you and your wife in your new-found joy. Most will want to visit mother and child in the hospital and bring gifts and ogle over, and maybe even cuddle, the baby.

Visitors are a good thing. They can break the monotony of the hospital routine for your wife and cheer her up if she's feeling down. It's great to see familiar faces, and a few flowers around the room certainly brighten things up. But visitors can become a real pain, particularly if you have a large family and loads of friends. The pain that they can become is mathematically correlated to the number of friends and relatives you have, the hours they choose to visit, the average length of time they stay, the volume of noise they produce and how hard it is to get rid of them.

The main problem is that visitors are exhausting. If you're really unlucky, your visitors will come in a constant stream, one after the other, like a pre-arranged tag-team. There will be an endless repetition of photos and questions and presents and chatter and laughter ... all day long. Mother and baby will end up wrung-out and irritated.

This is where you can help out. Be aware of your wife's needs. Maybe she and the baby don't want visitors straight away? Maybe your wife is exhausted and needs a bit of time to recover? If this is the case, tell your friends to hold off for a few days, and then try scheduling them so they all don't arrive at once. Also, discourage them from visiting outside of the assigned hours. This will ensure that both your wife and the baby get a decent rest.

Also be alert to your wife's desire for privacy. This may come as a surprise to you, but she may feel slightly uncomfortable about whipping out an engorged bosom for breastfeeding in front of all your cricket teammates, particularly if baby is being uncooperative.

Don't be afraid to tell your visitors – no matter who they are – when it's time to leave. If they don't take the hint, most Ward Sisters carry around an electric cattle prod which usually works quite well.

## GET READY – THEY'RE COMING HOME

Soon the time will come for your wife and baby to return home. If you're smart, there are a few things you can do that will help this grand homecoming run a little more smoothly. The general household routine will be pretty tumultuous for the next couple of months while you both get used to living with and caring for a little person in the house, so use the brief time you have alone to make some final preparations. This will get things off to a good start.

It's a great idea to have the house clean and tidy and 'ready for baby' on their return. Some balloons and flowers probably wouldn't go astray, either. Trust me when I say that family life will not get off on the right foot if your wife comes home to unmade beds, a pile of laundry, ironing, dirty dishes, dusty shelves and an expectation that it's her job to fix it all up.

An empty fridge will also not endear you to your wife, so make sure it is fully stocked. When my wife was still in hospital with Georgia, I went to the local butcher's shop and bought bulk supplies of ready-made stir-fries and marinades. I spent one morning in the kitchen cooking them all up and dishing them into disposable aluminium trays. I labelled them and filled the freezer to overflowing. Why not fill your fridge up with pastas and sauces? Mixed with freshly cooked vegetables and rice, and interspersed with other meals and the occasional takeaway, these supplies lasted us many weeks and helped especially on those days when things were a little hectic. (I am talking about decent food here, not high-fat high-salt cocktail franks, party pies and frozen pizzas.)

It is also important to get some sleep. If you are going to help out with the baby, you need to be rested and alert. All-night binges and TV marathons will just wear you down at a time when you need to be strong.

## THE CALM BEFORE THE STORM

Up to now, things have been kind of nice. You have probably been going to work and then popping into hospital for the occasional visit. You've been able to hold your baby for a little while, spend a bit of 'quality time' with your wife and then go back to the 'real world'. In fact, it's been almost like a holiday, living by yourself for the last couple of days. You could please yourself around the place, watch those DVDs you've been wanting to see, and eat spicy food.

This is the calm before the storm.

Your baby won't stay at the hospital forever. After a few days the doctor will say, 'Right, get out of here!' You pick up your wife, the baby, the bags, cards and flowers and drive home. The first thing you notice is that 'the two of you' are now 'the three of you'. There is another human being in the back of the car.

This is where all your training and reading and discussion and contemplation gets put to the acid test. This is where theory clashes headlong with reality. Life will never be the same again. So strap yourself in.

You are about to encounter the storm after the calm.

# CHAPTER FIVE

# SURVIVING AT HOME

*'One day, when your baby is seventeen and asking you for driving lessons and contraceptives, you'll look back on these times as "the easy years".'*

## LIFE BEYOND THE BIRTH

I have noticed something very interesting about weddings.

People who are engaged seem to spend every waking moment planning their 'big day'. For months and months – years, in some cases – their entire existence is directed at the thousands of small and intricate details that go into having the kind of fairytale wedding that the *Women's Weekly* ordains they should have.

And so comes the great event. After months of effort, everything goes smoothly. The wedding runs like clockwork and all is just perfect. In a flurry of rice and confetti, the bride and groom drive off into the sunset with a tremendous sigh of relief that it's all over.

Of course, it's not over at all – it's only just begun. My guess is that some couples spend so much time focusing on the wedding day itself that they forget to spare a thought for the more important part beyond ... their lives together. And so for some, the early days of marriage can come as a bit of a shock. Takes them by surprise, you might say.

The same applies to some people having a baby. So much time can be devoted to the labour itself – in books, conversations, birth classes, and so on – that some parents-to-be may neglect to look beyond, to the more important part which is to follow ... becoming parents and coping with a new addition to the home.

This is a fatal mistake. It is vital that you and your wife spend time *before* the birth thinking about and discussing life *beyond* the birth.

## THE TIMES, THEY ARE A' CHANGING

Do you remember your life before the baby came home? Life in your house with a newborn will not be the same as that. Babies are very demanding of time, and the little time that they do leave you is necessary for sleep. As such, there are many elements of your domestic life that you will need to adjust to your new situation. To help you understand what I mean, here is a list of things that become difficult when you have a baby living in your house. Note that I said 'difficult', not 'impossible'.

- listening to loud music;
- going shopping;
- washing the dishes;
- washing the car;
- washing clothes;
- hanging out clothes;
- ironing clothes;
- mowing the lawns;
- curling up with a good book;
- watching a DVD without interruption;

- having a relaxing evening together at home;
- having an in-depth adult conversation;
- going out;
- getting a good night's sleep;
- sleeping in;
- having sex on the spur of the moment;
- having sex even if you plan it carefully;
- even thinking about having sex;
- cooking;
- eating in peace;
- cleaning the house;
- practising your musical instrument;
- working at home (a fatal mistake); and
- writing a book.

The main consequence of this is that your home will look different to how it looked before. You may have a spacious and airy home; a home built for entertaining; a home filled with interesting and beautiful things. You may have an obsession with tidiness and cleanliness.

All this will have to be overcome.

For the next few years, your home will be a wasteland. Your windows will be smeared with greasy fingerprints. Sultanas and bananas will be squashed into the carpet. There will be a constant smell of urine and ammonia and every so often a hideous waft of something ghastly that you just can't locate. Every nook and cranny will become home to a million tiny building blocks, crusts, fluffy toys, little cars, broken crayons and doll's clothing. All drawers and cupboards below the four-foot level will at one time or another have their contents strewn randomly throughout every room.

I wish I could say something like, 'No, wait! Babies do actually make your life easier! You'll hardly notice they're there.'

But that would be a lie.

Babies are lots of work. Being an active and involved dad, you need to share in that work. I don't know what your domestic situation is; whether your wife is going to be a full-time homemaker or whether she's going back to work after a while. It may even be that you are so emancipated that *you* will be the one to stay home and look after the baby. Or the economic reality of today may mean that you both work full-time, in which case a lot of thought needs to be put into day care and job division. Whatever it is, though, you will need to discuss and plan your domestic duties and, once again, 'get your hands dirty'.

Of course, the work you do may not necessarily involve the baby directly. Regardless of what your domestic habits or roles have been in the past, if you are an I-mow-the-lawns-and-wash-the-car-and-the-wife-does-the-shopping,-washing,-tidying-and-cooking kind of guy, then you'll need to do a little bit of quick on-the-job training.

And whatever you do, never, ever, *ever* come home and say, 'Why is the house such a bloody mess? What's for dinner? Haven't you ironed my work shirts yet?' A tired woman with sore breasts is not to be crossed – that is, unless you want a nappy bucket tipped over your head.

## BOSOMS AND BOTTLES

There will always be topics over which people will argue:

- What is the superior football code?
- Jesus Christ: liar, lunatic or Lord?
- What really happened to Harold Holt?
- Who was the best Batman: Adam West, Michael Keaton, George Clooney, Val Kilmer or Christian Bale?
- Should Australia become a republic?
- Is Elvis really working at a hamburger joint in town?

And this golden gem:

- Should a mother bottle-feed or breastfeed?

The feeding of babies is a surprisingly contentious issue. Advocates of either method can become very fiery about their beliefs. There are two enemy camps: The Bottle Alliance versus United Breastfeeders, and each side has its own support organisations, newsletters and surveillance satellites.

Given that most shelf space in the bookshop parenting section is dedicated to feeding, it would be ludicrous of me to attempt to go into detail about feeding options. But just for the heck of it, here are the main arguments:

Breastfeeding:

- is natural;
- uses 'live' milk, full of antibodies which strengthen the baby's immune system;
- encourages closeness and bonding between mother and child;
- splits the mother's nipples in half;
- can be awkward in public for some mothers (even though in this day and age, it shouldn't be);
- can be frustrating and time-consuming;
- can't be done by you, the bloke;
- can be affected by the mother's diet (onions, nicotine, garlic, etc.);
- can utilise bottle technology for babysitting purposes; and
- is cheap (free!).

Bottle-feeding:

- is not done by any other mammal on the planet;
- can be done by men;
- is not 'live' from the mother, but is derived from cow's or soy milk and supplemented with various vitamins and minerals;
- keeps the mother's nipples in one piece;

- means mucking around with bottle kits and sterilisers;
- can be more convenient for working couples;
- is easier to prepare for babysitters; and
- costs money.

You can tell that I have a personal bias towards breastfeeding. This is for two main reasons. Firstly, *Choice* magazine says, and I quote, 'Breast is Best'. Secondly, my cousin is a lactation consultant and I'll never hear the end of it if I don't fly the breastfeeding flag, so to speak.

Either way, your role is important. Newborns feed about every four hours, twenty-four hours a day. This means getting up regularly throughout the night. If your wife breastfeeds, you can get the baby for her and put it back to bed. If your baby is being bottle-fed, work out a roster and split the workload

You can also help by burping your baby. Because they guzzle and suck so greedily, babies often swallow air while feeding. This sits in their stomachs and causes them great discomfort, which leads to crying, which in turn causes stress, tension and sleeplessness in their parents (see below).

To burp your baby, hold it upright with its head over your shoulder and gently pat its back while you sing a song. After a while the baby will come forth with a deafening peal of thunder – the kind of burp you'd expect to hear from a beer-swilling truckie. It is also usually accompanied by a hefty curdled-milk projectile spew, although this normally only happens when you've got a good shirt on. If you ever play rub-noses with your baby after they have had a feed, make sure your wife is videoing you, because then she can capture the moment when the baby projectiles into your mouth, and you can submit it as an award-winning clip to one of those funny home video shows.

If your wife decides breastfeeding is the way to go, fantastic. But if bottle-feeding is your option – if, say, your wife is sick or under stress, or if the baby is unwilling to go on her breast – that's fine too. Babies are nourished by formulae everywhere in the world, every day of the year. So read some books, talk with your wife, discuss it with your doctor and the hospital lactation consultants to work out which option is best for your wife and your baby.

And two other things. I shouldn't need to say these, but I will ... just in case.

- Don't ever use breastmilk or formulae in tea or coffee. Just trust me on this.
- Some women lactate with only the slightest prompting. Never, *ever* say to a breastfeeding mother stuff like, 'Hey, so you're breastfeeding, huh? Wow, it's really physically intimate isn't it? How amazing to have your own body giving nourishment to your child, to see the baby's mouth on your breast and to hear the *schloop schloop* noise as your milk flows. It must be a wonderfully satisfying sensation ...' They will suddenly develop two large wet patches on their blouse, and they will not be happy.

## THE CRYING GAME

I never knew that babies cry as much as they do. I think that is because, as a child, the only baby I ever saw was Jesus in nativity drawings on Christmas cards. Have you ever seen a Christmas card where Jesus is crying? No! He is always asleep. What a deception! (Actually, I have friends who believe that this in itself is actually proof that Jesus was the Son of God. But I'm sidetracking.)

We have a neighbour who has a faulty car alarm. It goes off at all hours of the day and night, for hours on end. *Wwwaaaaaeeeeerrrrr. Wwwaaaaaeeeeerrrrr.* It is an excruciating klaxon wail that goes on and on and on until all the people in my street are driven to the point of insanity. When it starts up, I feel like going over to his house and yelling at him and smashing his car with a hammer. Now *that* would be something to get alarmed over.

Imagine having a car alarm that lives in your own house. It goes off regularly during the day and night. And imagine that you have to pick the car alarm up and cuddle it and kiss it. You sing to it and mumble soothing words and, guess what?! It just gets louder! That's what a baby in full cry mode is like. Yelling and hammers are definitely out of the question.

Babies cry. That's their job. They're particularly good at it. In fact, some babies love to cry. And when they cry, they are not doing it because they want to sound nice. A baby's cry is most often loud, incessant and very irritating. That's what it's supposed to be like. It's an attention-getter. It says, 'Hey, you, come here! I want something!'

You see, when you or I want something, we go and get it. If we feel uncomfortable, we fix ourselves up. If we're thirsty, we go to the fridge. If we're hungry, we dial for pizza. However, babies can't do this. Their single form of communication is crying. So they'll cry if they are lonely, thirsty or hungry, if they are cold or hot, if they are tired or wet, if the TV is too loud or the light is too bright. They'll cry because it was nicer in the womb, or because they don't like the way you decorated their nursery.

In short, babies cry about just about anything. Of course the problem with this is that all beasts – from the Himalayan rock slug to *Homo sapiens* – have an instinctive protective response to the crying of their offspring. So you must be careful: you don't want to mollycoddle the baby; you don't want to treat every whimper like a national emergency. If you spoil your baby it'll end up being one of those ratty kids whom you see at hamburger restaurants squealing, 'I want fries! I want a party hat! I hate pickles! I want one of those plastic cartoon character figurines!' But on the other hand, you don't want to be one of those parents featured on the seven o'clock news because they let their baby scream for two days running.

The great fun that lies ahead for you is the guessing game that you will get to play trying to work out what is 'wrong' with your child. You cannot win this game. You see, some babies cry just because they damn well feel like it. And sometimes there is nothing you can do about it.

And then, of course, there is the arch nemesis of parents everywhere: COLIC.

Colic (translated from the German word *Karlech*, meaning 'scream of death') is one of those things which occur even though no one can explain why – like yawns, sudden biro leaks and reality-television shows.

Colic is a pattern of unstoppable screaming at the same time every day, usually in the early evening. These sessions can last up to a few hours per go and may continue for a few months at a time.

When this behaviour starts, it's best to consult your doctor just to confirm that the crying isn't caused by something more serious. Apart from that, you just have to do your best to cope with the noise. See if it's feed-time, check the baby's temperature, cuddle them, talk to them or change them. You can make them more comfortable by massaging them, shoving a dummy in their mouth, or rocking their cradle. If that doesn't work, get a rug and go sit in the garden, or take the baby for a walk in the pram. The screaming never sounds as bad outside the claustrophobic confines of your loungeroom. Why not go to a busy shopping centre? It won't necessarily quiet the baby down, but at least you can make all the other bastards suffer as much as you are.

If all else fails, you can always sing. When singing, avoid red-blooded renditions of 'Here we go. Here we go. Here we go!' and 'It's a long way to the top if you wanna rock 'n' roll'. Make it gentle, soft and soothing. If you don't know any tunes, make one up – your baby won't know the difference. In fact, you can sing any song you know, as long as you sing it slowly, softly and melodically. Sway back and forth in time to your song and tap a 4/4 beat on the baby's bottom.

This whole crying game needs a lot of patience. A sense of humour doesn't go astray, either. The problem for us blokes, as my mother constantly reminds me, is that:

*Patience is a virtue, bless it if you can*
*Always in a woman, never in a man.*

Yeah, great. Thanks, Mum. What can I say? Good luck. One day, when your baby is seventeen and asking you for driving lessons and contraceptives, you'll look back on these times as 'the easy years'.

Of course, most of us can cope with crying babies when it's a sunny day and the birds are singing and we are feeling alert and strong.

The real test comes at night when you want to sleep.

For many years, political dictators and dungeon-masters have been developing and refining their methods of torture. They have used hot pokers, thumbscrews, the rack, Brahms's 'Lullaby' and screenings of Kevin Costner movies to make their victims beg for mercy. But there's one form of torture that is used more widely and more effectively than all the others.

Sleep deprivation.

Deprive a man of sleep and he will undergo a Jekyll and Hyde transformation of epic proportions. A normally placid and pleasant Mr Average can quickly turn into a short-tempered, bleary-eyed, babbling fool, then a rabid, angry and irrational beast. All of a sudden, his whole life is a mess. Unshaven and unkempt, he'll be aggressive to workmates and fall asleep on the job. He can no longer construct a fluent sentence. His eyelids feel like they are made of lead.

The problem is that babies don't live by the clock or the sun. They don't have the same culturally entrenched ideas about keeping 'polite hours'. The immediate consequence of this is that they wake up a lot during the night and need to be tended to: fed, burped, changed, rocked to sleep. It's also likely that there'll be a good deal of screaming thrown in for good measure. And when a baby gets a good howl happening in the quiet of the night, it's like a 747 thundering down your hallway.

*Brahms was a sadist …*

I'm not just talking about waking up once for a few minutes in the middle of the night. I know of a couple who called their son The Screamer. He only slept for four hours a day!

Gasp! Shock! Snooze! I hear you cry. *Four hours*, did you say? That's inhuman! You're right. It is inhuman. But that's not the worst part. You see, he didn't sleep four hours in one hit. That was merely his cumulative total. The four hours were made up of occasional twenty-minute snoozes! Meditate on this and you start to realise the impact a baby can have on your household.

Of course, I'm painting a bit of a pessimistic picture. Your baby could alternatively be a marathon sleeper, sleeping as many as eighteen hours in twenty-four. Its cry might only be a barely audible whimper. You may have what is commonly referred to in fathering circles as 'a really good baby'. If you do, count yourself lucky.

My guess is that, historically, Dad went to bed at the normal time and any nocturnal activity of the waking-up-and-stuffing-around-with-the-baby-in-the-freezing-cold-dead-of-night variety definitely fell under Mum's job description. But you need to remember that you are into shared parenting; active fathering.

This is the time when you need to remember that if your wife is at home, she works all day too and probably never gets a decent break from the baby and has to put up with that screaming all the time.

So, how can *you* help when the baby starts choir practice at 2 am?

When Rachael was born, I thought I had a pretty foolproof escape clause from any nocturnal activity. My logic was that since I was lacking in the necessary equipment – i.e. one pair of milk-swollen breasts – I was of no use whatsoever and could therefore just roll over and go back to sleep. Of course, I watched my wife gradually turn into a zombie with dark eyes and a blank expression, only capable of monosyllabic conversation.

This 'It's not my problem' approach is definitely a bad one. (But in my defence, I *did* try to help. Whenever Meredith was up feeding, I would roll over and keep her side of the bed warm.)

When Georgia was born, I was guilt-ridden and vowed to go fifty-fifty with my wife. Whenever she got up, I too got up to put on the heater, make hot chocolate and keep her company. This had two immediate effects. Firstly, my presence and talking prevented Georgia from nodding off, which kept us up much longer than necessary. Secondly, we both ended up as zombies with dark eyes and blank expressions, capable only of monosyllabic conversation. And it really is quite embarrassing to fall asleep at your desk in front of a class of Year 10 students and then wake up only to realise that you are dribbling and all the kids are staring at you.

So this 'We'll share the torment together' approach is equally inadequate.

But what's the answer?

Without wanting to sound trite, the answer lies in a balance between the two approaches. It's no good one person doing all the work, but it's no good both of you doing all the work, either. Like I said before, parenting is a team game, so share the responsibilities as much as you can. If your baby is being breastfed, play the delivery boy and get the baby from the cot and bring it to Mum in bed. You can take turns in burping the baby and singing it off to sleep. This approach worked quite well when we had Matilda. Meredith still did all the feeding, but I tried to help with the burping, settling and dummy patrol. When it's not your turn, the best thing you can do is sleep.

In the harsh light of day, though, I rarely lived up to the grandiose expectations I frequently set for myself. If you are in a situation where you are doing everything fifty-fifty with your wife, well you're a better man than I am, Mr Din. For most of us, the fact is that our wives still draw the short straw.

Discussion and job-sharing really are the keys to coping. When your wife is fed up, send her out to a movie or for a walk or to a friend's place. And if you're fed up, be sensible enough to accept a break. In BC times (Before Children), whenever I had a spare moment I would fill it with guitar playing or book reading or weight training. In AD times (After Delivery), with a baby in the house, my most favoured activity quickly became catching up on sleep.

But of course it's fine for me to talk about 'discussion' and 'job-sharing' as if they're the answer to all your night-time troubles. The reality of getting up to a crying baby may be somewhat different. And it's only at this point that I warn you about something ...

Stuffing around with a baby, especially in the middle of the night, can be really frustrating. The crying is harder to cope with because all is quiet and this only exacerbates the shrill pitch of the baby's cry. It's dark and still and you feel like you're the only person on Earth who's awake. You feel even more lonely and isolated because often the only company you have in the wee hours are the people in infommercials for ab-workers, low-fat barbecue hotplates and indestructible sunglasses. And that's enough to drive anybody crazy.

After a while it becomes very easy to lose your temper. I had read about this in books, but because I am a mature and well-adjusted bloke, I knew that this would not be a problem for me. Right?

Wrong.

This fact dawned on me in the early hours one morning as I was playing a lengthy game called 'putting Georgia back to bed after a midnight snack'. Every night Meredith and I played this game. That night it was my turn. I stood there next to her cot, trying to rock her off to sleep (Georgia that is, not Meredith). Pretty soon I was fighting to keep my eyes open and a while later I was leaning against the wall while mumbling some inane lullaby. Before I knew it my face was sliding down the wallpaper and then I came to, huddled semi-naked and freezing on the floor. Eventually, after what seemed like hours but were probably only minutes, she dozed off. I then had to endure the agony of trying to lower her into the cot and get my arm out without waking her, a sensation best illustrated in action movies when a sweaty government agent has to carefully remove an incredibly sensitive beeping electronic thing from a metal housing and if he so much as breathes too heavily, then his arm will jolt and a warning light will start flashing and ten seconds later there'll be a nuclear explosion, killing him and everyone in a twenty-kilometre radius.

Mission accomplished, I spent what seemed like twenty minutes sneaking back down the corridor to my bedroom, tiptoeing like a kung-fu master walking on rice paper. I made it to within a few tantalising feet of the warmth of my bed before I hit that creaky floorboard. Then she cranked up again.

She had just been fed, so she wasn't hungry.

She had just been changed, so she wasn't wet.

She was wrapped in a blanket, so she wasn't cold.

So I went back and started gently rocking the cot. I mean, I was doing it by the book. But she was still screaming like I was taunting her with red-hot irons. I started singing. And rocking. Singing and rocking.

This had worked well before, but on this occasion ... it didn't.

I started feeling angry. It was dark. I was tired. My best attempts at baby-soothing had been frustrated. Her scream was deafening. My feet were cold. My eyes were sore. So I rocked harder. It still didn't work.

Then all of a sudden, I felt like a volcano of frustration was welling up inside me. I wanted to bang the cot hard and run outside and rip up trees by their trunks and smash armoured vehicles with my fists, just like the Incredible Hulk. I was losing control. Somewhere in the back of my brain, an alarm light started flashing. So I backed outta there and went and splashed some water on my face and took a few deep breaths. Then I took Georgia into the loungeroom, put the TV and the heater on and started the singing/rocking routine again. Being in a warm, bright room made me wake up a bit and feel better and, more importantly, cope a whole lot better.

You should be aware of this nocturnal frustration. It is real. There are ways of coping, however. Perhaps you could put on some nice music and make a cup of tea. I know a couple who used to put their baby in its car capsule and go for a drive. The noise and rhythm of the car soothed the baby and sent it off to sleep. (Just make sure *you* don't fall asleep at the wheel.) Another couple I know get up, put their baby in a sling and vacuum the house. The noise drowns out the screams, the house gets clean and the baby is eventually soothed by the rhythm. What more could you ask for?

If you start 'losing it', put the baby in its crib where it can't hurt itself and go back to bed, or get in the shower. If things are really bad, don't be afraid or embarrassed to phone up a compliant friend or relative to come and help you out. Even chatting to a phone counsellor at 3 am can lift your spirits.

Of course, it all depends on whether your baby is a dozer or a screamer and how well you and your wife handle sleep deprivation. But have the attitude of helping. Take it in turns to deal with the baby, and discuss what suits your situation best.

And, good luck, mate. You'll need it.

## SIDS

Once a year, you probably notice something strange going on. As you go about your business of the day in the street and shops and at work, you observe that people are wearing plastic red noses. Even buses and public buildings and landmarks are decorated with a giant red proboscis. This is not some public celebration of the life of Bozo the Clown, but rather a popular fundraising and awareness day in relation to SIDS.

SIDS stands for Sudden Infant Death Syndrome.

The academic definition of SIDS, defined at the 2004 Australian SIDS Pathology Workshop, is:

*The sudden and unexpected death of an infant under one year of age, with onset of the lethal episode apparently occurring during sleep, that remains unexplained after a thorough investigation including performance of a complete autopsy, and review of the circumstances of death and the clinical history.*

What this means in layman's terms is that some babies die in their sleep and no one knows why.

SIDS is the most common form of death of babies between one month and one year of age, with the ages of one to six months accounting for over 80 per cent of these. However, a combination of intensive medical research and large-scale public-awareness campaigns has meant that since 1991, when the *Reducing the Risk of SIDS Program* was introduced in Australia, the number of deaths has dropped by 70 per cent. While still a tragic figure, the current rate of death from SIDS has dropped to about one in two thousand.

While no one knows what causes SIDS, research has provided us with practices that will reduce the chance of SIDS occurring. These are good for you to know, and it is certainly worth your while doing some more extensive reading on this subject. Brochures are readily available from birth classes, hospitals and early childhood centres, and there are many websites that provide specific details and advice.

So what can you do to reduce the chance of your baby dying of SIDS?

In the first place, babies should sleep on their backs in a cot that is free of junk. There should be no electric blankets, water bottles, pillows, fluffy toys, bumpers, quilts, doonas or any other loose bedding or toys in there. A baby should be tucked in securely, with its face clearly uncovered. A fitted baby sleeping bag is ideal. The baby's feet should be at the base of the cot so that it has little chance of burrowing down under the covers.

Smoking is also a highly correlated factor, with babies of smokers being twenty to forty times more likely to die of SIDS than babies of non-smokers. So if you're a smoker, there's no time like now to give up.

If you are having a babysitter look after your baby, make sure that they are clear on the above information. Things may well have been different in Grandma's day and she is probably not as up to speed as you are on current SIDS advice. ('Listen, deary, I used to pop you face-down and bury you in your cot with your favourite doona and all your teddy bears, and you couldn't have been happier!')

## DO NOT FEED THE ANIMAL

If you stick your finger in your baby's mouth you will notice that it feels more like a mullet than a tiger. There are no teeth. But it doesn't stay like that forever. At anywhere around the six-month mark, the first of twenty little white splinters will drive their way through your baby's gums. This is their first set of teeth, which they will have for about six years.

This has many immediate effects:

- Your baby will drool. There will be a continuous river of saliva running from its lower lip down to its navel, giving your baby a glistening appearance.

- Your baby may be very uncomfortable. It may be whingey and miserable and have difficulty sleeping sometimes.
- If your wife breastfeeds, you will hear her scream intermittently as the baby's carnivorous instincts impact upon her nipples.
- The baby will produce nappies of such suffocating intensity and revolting consistency that you will wish you were dead rather than changing them.
- If your baby bites you, it will hurt.

Now this is all part of the natural order, because a newborn baby only drinks milk and so doesn't need teeth. But over the course of its first year, your baby will start its journey towards real food. This process is called weaning, whereby its milk intake is lowered and solids are gradually phased in.

(I use the term 'solids' here very loosely. To me, a solid is a rump steak, a caesar salad with a bowl of chips and some pork crackling on the side. To baby-food manufacturers, however, a solid is a banana that has spent an hour in a blender.)

The latest health guidelines recommend that a baby should be breastfed exclusively for its first six months, before weaning begins. But don't expect it to take place overnight. It is a slow process. Be guided by your baby – if it shows interest in foods, or if it isn't gaining in weight as it ought to be, or if it has reached six months of age, start on solids. To begin, only one or two teaspoons of food should be offered once a day for the first couple of weeks and then you build from there. These early foods should be bland, wet and slushy, like rice cereal, fruit purée, gels and sieved vegetables. Don't give too much food at any one sitting – breastmilk should still be its main source of nutrition up to six months and even beyond; and introduce new foods slowly, feeding each new type for two or three days running to check for possible allergic reactions before introducing the next food.

And it's also around this teething time that you can introduce rusks, which are little sticks of flavoured concrete that babies use to sharpen their teeth on so when they bite you, they get a better response.

With this onset of teeth, your baby can start on foods of a more resilient consistency. You can throw your whole dinner into a blender and give them a semi-solid goulash of homemade baby fare. Later on you can introduce them to actual pieces of bread, cheese, fish (boned), chicken, vegies, hamburger, fruits ... in fact, pretty well anything off your dinner plate will do, as long as it's not vindaloo, chilli con carne or jalapeno burritos.

One of the problems with introducing solids is that babies like to experiment with their food. This usually involves putting it into their mouth, chewing it, spitting it out, picking it up, rubbing it into their clothes, throwing some of it into your face, running it through their hair and then putting it back in their mouth again. Don't be too concerned if only a small amount of food actually gets into your baby's mouth. Recent university tests have found that babies actually get the nutrition out of their food via the process of osmosis, whereby the vitamins and minerals soak directly through their skin.

The trouble is, this process tends to make a bit of a mess. For this reason, the only safe place to feed a baby is in one of those nuclear-shielded handling rooms where everything is done by robotic arms. But given that you probably don't have such a facility at your place, you could instead feed your baby over lino tiles or in the centre of a plastic tablecloth. Even then, you will still find morsels of food splattered on the ceiling on the other side of the room.

To protect the baby's clothing, many people use bibs. These are cheap, which means all your friends will buy you ten packets each as a present and you'll need a separate cupboard to store them in. (The bibs, not your friends.) But bibs are peculiar things: unfortunately, they don't work. Babies will get food down their sleeves and in their socks, and no tiny piece of cloth with cute bunny prints is going to stop them. So not only will you need to wash their clothes (which you would have done anyway), you'll also need to wash hundreds of bibs as well, increasing your washing load by 200 per cent.

The only outfit that will protect your baby's clothing is either a full-length wetsuit or a radiation suit.

## NAPPIES

To many men, fatherhood is a scary prospect. They are nervous about all the awesome changes and responsibilities that accompany family life. There are also new financial pressures, a major change to the daily timetable, lack of sleep and more household chores. And if you are an obsessive worry-wart of epic proportions, questions like 'Which high school will be best for my daughter?', 'What happens if my son crashes the car?' and 'What wedding reception venue will give me the best value for money?' may soon begin to weigh heavily upon your mind.

But to most men there is one thing that is scarier than all these other worries put together.

It is worse than any horror film.

It is the stuff of which nightmares are made.

It is ... nappies.

Festering, smouldering ones.

About twelve a day ... if you're lucky.

Nappies really are incredible things. Like ants, babies can carry around in their nappies over one hundred times their own body weight. This is frightening, because then they need to be changed.

In the classic film *Three Men and a Baby*, when Tom Selleck is faced with the prospect of changing another 'diaper', he offers his good mate Steve Guttenburg a thousand dollars to do it for him.

Of course, this sounds very funny. Ha ha. But you will soon realise that Selleck's bribery is quite understandable – some would even say quite good value for money.

Toying with nappies is not something that you will find as pleasant as toying with a nice red wine, for example. I found this out many years ago when I stayed with a friend who had a six-month-old baby. I was a 'nappy virgin' and had never experienced a real live 3-D nappy-changing with full smell-o-rama before. After witnessing the event, I never wanted to experience one again. I immediately went into 'nappy shock', also known in psychological circles as 'post-nappy traumatic syndrome'. I lay prostrate on my friend's front steps, sweaty-faced and gasping for air.

He laughed at me and said, 'It's OK, mate. It's always bad with somebody else's kid. I couldn't change any other babies but my own. But your own kids – no worries.'

I drew much reassurance from this, despite the fact that it turned out to be a complete lie. As far as I'm concerned, nappies are nappies, no matter who they come from.

Many years later, when my wife was pregnant, another friend told us that changing a newborn baby's nappy was like a 'walk in the roses'. This also turned out to be a lie. I've never smelled a rose that made me dry-retch.

And it's no use thinking that you can make it through the early years of your baby's life without changing one. You can't. This is the enlightened twenty-first century and if you want to experience fatherhood in all its glory, then you have to 'get your hands dirty' (and trust me, when changing nappies you *will* get your hands dirty). Being a dad is more than doing all the fun jobs like playing in the backyard and giving paternal lectures. Nappy-changing, despite the opinion of many, is not an innately maternal pastime. Your baby is going to go through thousands of nappies in its first years, amounting to several hundred kilograms of solid waste. Your cunning plan to conveniently not be around at nappy-changing time is simply not going to work. So don't pike out.

My first nappies were memorable.

I have always prided myself on my fortitude and steel stomach. After all, I do have a St John's Ambulance Certificate and have seen every Arnie film ever made. But I went to jelly in the face of my first nappies. In fact, I dry-retched. I didn't realise it at the time, but these were to be the first in a long line of reverse peristalsis experiences in the presence of Nappies From Hell.

Over its first few days, the baby's nappies contain a disgusting greeny–black, sticky, festering, stenchy mess called meconium. (Picture it basically as tar.) This is the digested goop that the baby has swallowed in the womb. (Uurrgghh, I'm gagging just thinking about it.) Don't let it come into contact with your skin. That stuff just doesn't come off.

Once the baby's system is cleaned out and the breastmilk has worked its way through, the nappies improve markedly, in a relative sense anyway. For the first few months the baby will produce a seemingly impossible volume of wet, sloppy, gooey fluid, the kind you'd expect as the result of having a purely liquid diet. (If meconium is tar, then picture milk-fed nappies as being like lumpy gravy.)

But once the baby starts eating solids (especially meat), then you're in real trouble. That's when you have to deal with fair dinkum solid crap, perfectly moulded into rhomboidal patties in the airspace formed by the baby's buttocks and nappy. These craps are so unique in chemistry that they have their own label in the periodic table of elements: 113 Excretium (Ex), with an atomic weight of 272.03.

Although difficult at first, after a while you get used to it. A veteran of three babies, I can now change the most nuclear nappy with my bare hands – in the dark, even, although that's generally not a good idea.

When cleaning your baby's bum, use disposable moist towelettes or cotton wool balls and water to wipe away the slimy poop that is smeared on its skin. Some bits might need a bit more elbow grease because if you've left it too long, little poopy flecks will have dried out and set like concrete. If the bum is red and rashy, you can apply some barrier cream or nappy rash cream to help soothe and protect the irritated skin.

Apart from that, when changing nappies here are two helpful tips.

## RULE ONE: THE NAPPY MUST NOT COME OFF UNDER ANY CIRCUMSTANCES.

A loose nappy can drop off of its own accord. Older babies can also work out how to take them off. Use electrical tape, an arc welder, superglue – whatever it takes to make the nappies secure. If you don't, your baby will use the chunky stuff as paint ... or worse. Trust me. It's not easy bonding with a baby who has crap all around its mouth.

## RULE TWO: HOLD YOUR BREATH WHILE CHANGING.

Fumes from nappies are poisonous. NASA scientists actually use nappy fumes to simulate the atmosphere of Mars in their astronaut training program. If you happen to suck in a lungful without protective breathing apparatus, you can be rendered unconscious and keel over.

In your role as nappy changer, you have basically five choices:

*it's really hard to bond ...*

## Choice 1: Disposable Nappies

Environmental organisations tell us that disposables have the same half-life as toxic waste. Which is not surprising, considering that nappies *contain* the chemical equivalent of toxic waste. They will still be intact and lethal at the local rubbish dump when your children are having children of their own. So if you're green, disposables are not for you.

Also, babies go through nappies about as quickly as you can put them on. At first you will use about twelve a day. This is going to cost you a tidy sum, especially considering that babies are in nappies for about two years. And if your garbage is only collected once a week, you will soon find that the sauna-like effect of the wheely bin on the seventy or so little packets will lead to a marital dispute as to who gets to put the bin out. And the garbos will probably hate you too.

In addition, some parents don't like the chemical smell and feel of some disposables.

And in case you think that buying disposable nappies is easy, think again. There are more varieties of nappies than there are types of dog food – all with computer-designed, colour-coded, sex-differentiated, scientifically proven features which will take your baby's bum through the next millennium. There are disposables for newborns, infants, crawlers, toddlers and juniors, nappies for boys, nappies for girls and even 'non-ballooning' secure nappies for the swimming pool.

Of course, disposables are by definition *disposable*. Herein lies their main attraction. They may be expensive, but they are quick and convenient to use. When they're 'soiled', the responsible and hygienic thing to do is to scrape the gunk off into the toilet before discarding the nappy. (That stuff shouldn't go to the tip, it should go to the sewerage plant.) Then you simply wrap them up and throw them away. This is particularly advantageous if you are out for the day and don't wish to carry around a plastic bag of fermenting sludge. So if you are not philosophically opposed to non-biodegradable nappies and if you have a healthy bank account, disposables are for you.

## Choice 2: Traditional Cloth Nappies

Ah yes, just like mother used to use on you. Some parents find cloth nappies fiddly and time-consuming. Others like the feel and smell of the cotton and consider it a more natural alternative than disposables.

Initially, you need to buy a couple of large buckets with lids and a stack of about forty nappies and some plastic pants. After emptying a soiled nappy, throw it in the bucket for a soak in sterilising fluid. (As these are germ killers, they are not particularly good for the environment so if you are on your own septic, avoid emptying the bucket down the plug hole.) After an overnight soak, throw the nappies in your washing machine with a good washing powder. Hanging the nappies out in the sun will bleach even the most lurid yellow ones white. It sounds complex and time-consuming, but once you have a regular system up and running it's really quite simple.

Until recently, nappies were held together with big safety pins. This was a nightmare, particularly when the pin burst through the cloth and speared deep under your fingernail. ('Infection? Let *me* tell *you* about infection!')

Fortunately, some bright spark invented a three-pronged clip that serves the same purpose as pins. Called the 'snappy', this is widely available and is considerably easier, quicker and less painful to use. That is, unless you tread on one with bare feet.

## Choice 3: The Nappy Combo

No, not a new meal deal from your local hamburger restaurant. ('Would you like any desserts with your nappy, Sir?') Many people use a combination of both disposable and cloth nappies. With this you get the best of both worlds: cloth nappies during the day and around the house, disposable nappies at night and for trips away from home.

## Choice 4: Nappy Service

Tom Selleck should have thought about this! While you still have to deal with the stuff at the bum end, with a nappy service you don't have to muck about with scraping or washing the nappies themselves. For a reasonable sum you can have someone drop off a giant bag of fresh, clean nappies at your front door once or twice a week. At the same time they'll take away a giant bag of sodden, sludgy ones. (Of course, this gets more fun as the week goes on and the bag fills up – particularly in summer. This is also a great way of getting back at neighbours you don't like who live downwind from you. Even better, it keeps door-to-door salesmen and various religious cults away.)

If you have a friend or relative who wants to buy you a present but isn't sure what to get you, a couple of weeks' worth of nappy service will be a gift you'll really appreciate. Trust me.

And don't worry. You'll soon get over your reservations about the fact that the nappy you're putting on your beautiful baby has been crapped in by over two hundred other babies in your suburb.

## Choice 5: Your baby wears no nappy at all

Unfortunately, babies do not have the ablutionary graces that we adults have developed over the years. The most pressing consequence of this is that for the next couple of years, they'll 'go' *where* they want, *when* they want, and they'll do it *often*. Somebody's got to clean it up because if you don't, your baby will eat it. We have (shall we say *earthy*) friends who decided not to restrict their baby by having it wear nappies. They wanted it to be free and didn't like the idea of it having to be sitting in a bag of its own waste. Nice in theory, but the short version is that their carpet and soft-furnishings are in a state of soggy ruin and we try not to visit them anymore.

Choice 5 is stupid. Don't even consider it.

No matter what option you choose, however, invest in a nappy-changing outfit. A wetsuit, scuba tank, welding mask, blacksmith's gloves and a wooden spoon will do you nicely.

## SPLISH SPLASH

Babies have to be washed. If you don't wash them, they will start to smell and you won't like having them around.

While you may think it the most easy option, hosing your baby down in the backyard is generally considered to be unacceptable, particularly in winter. One easy option is the frequently used 'top 'n' tail'. This is where you just wash the baby's face and bum with a flannel. If you use the same flannel for both bits, it's a good idea to wash the baby's face first.

Every so often, though, you do need to give your baby a bath. You can do this in a 'safe' sink (a sink free of taps sticking out at skull-cracking angles and with no danger of hot taps coming on), or preferably in a baby bath like the one I told you about in Chapter Three, placed either up on a sturdy bench or table, or on the floor. If you're really game, you can take them in the big bath with you.

You must be very careful with the temperature of the water. A baby bath should be pleasantly warm, not hot. It is easy to scald a baby. They do not have the same tolerance for hot water that you enjoy when you have a nice, hot, relaxing steamy soak. (If you have the baby in the bath with you, the temperature should be set for the baby, not for you.) But how do you get the temperature right? Some friends of mine actually use a baby bath thermometer which floats in the bath and turns different colours if the bath is too hot or too cold. Many people say that the best way to test a bath is to splash some water on your wrist. Others say to dip your elbow into the water. (Since when has the human elbow been held in regard for its sensitivity? My elbow is as tough as elephant's hide and has the sensitivity of concrete. I found the best way was to run the bath and stick my head under the surface. Sure, it was messy, but I quickly started getting the temperature right!)

*Never leave the baby alone in the bath*, not even for a second. Every year, babies drown because Mum or Dad quickly went to answer the phone or even just turned around to get a towel. (Take the phone off the hook and get all your stuff ready in front of you before you even start.) Babies can drown in just 4 centimetres of water, and all it takes is the time for them to draw a single breath. So once again, *never leave the baby alone in the bath*, not even for a second. You also need to take care to support the baby's lolling head in the early months.

It is important, too, that you set up the bath and dressing area with everything you need *before* you bring the baby into the picture. That way, you don't have to leave your baby alone on the change-table or whatever while you go hunting for this or that.

When dressing a baby after its bath, get the nappy on first, particularly if your baby is a boy. Boys have an instinctive defence system, linked to their penis, which transforms this organ into a high-pressure rotational urine squirter. This squirter has its own locking mechanism and is constantly aimed at your face. Don't say I didn't warn you.

## OUT AND ABOUT

It's hard to be a social butterfly and a new parent at the same time. With the baby's patterns of feeding, sleeping and soiling nappies, going out isn't as easy as it used to be. A simple thing like visiting friends or going to the shops becomes an epic task. Outings like an afternoon at the cricket, a spur-of-the-moment movie or a weekend sail on the harbour with your wife become a veritable impossibility.

Not that your life comes to a complete standstill; it's more like a radical screeching down through the gears. Your social calendar will need to adjust to your changed home environment.

This doesn't mean that you have to make like Rapunzel and stay locked indoors. It's just that outings become a little more complicated and require a bit more thought and planning than they used to.

In your pre-baby years, going out was a relatively simple thing. More often than not you could make it out of the house in seconds. Grab your car keys and wallet, brush your hair – thirty seconds, tops. It doesn't work like this anymore. Operation Desert Storm was easier to co-ordinate and initiate than Operation Getting Out the Front Door. This is organisation on a grand scale.

The baby has to be put in a clean nappy, dressed, rugged up and finally held. This then reduces the holder to one arm. The bag has to be packed with a blanket, extra nappies, plastic bags, bottles, dummies, creams, gels, a change of clothes, fluffy toys with jingly bells, and so on. The car capsule has to be refitted and the pram folded into the boot. The travel cot needs to be packed down and squashed into whatever available space you have left. (By the way, most TAFEs offer Engineering diplomas specialising in travel-cot construction.)

Once supply lines have been established, there's the plan of attack to consider. If you're going to your mother-in-law's for lunch, for example, make your estimated time of departure half an hour earlier than normal. That way you'll ensure that you only miss the first course. Because just when you're ready to go, you can bet that your baby will need a feed.

And if it's a really big night – somewhere where your baby just can't go – you need to start planning weeks in advance. A babysitter needs to be organised, and if your wife is breastfeeding, an adequate supply of breast milk expressed and frozen.

One final word of warning about going out and about. Many modern shopping centres, hamburger restaurants and airports have 'unisex' baby-changing facilities. But every so often you will find yourself stuck somewhere where the baby change-rooms are in the women's toilets. So if you are trapped in a large suburban shopping centre and your baby develops a severe case of 'toxic nappy', you have only two options:

## Option 1
Assert your rights as a modem man and barge into the women's toilet. At best, you'll get the baby changed before anyone notices. At worst, you'll get beaten up by a pack of grandmothers and quite possibly get arrested.

## Option 2
Squat down on the floor, lay out a mat and change the nappy in the middle of a busy department-store walkway. I know a guy who actually does this! Interestingly, it won't take long for your 'nappy terrorism' to make an impact. Depending on how bad the nappy is, architects will probably be brought in within the week, and a month later, after substantial structural renovation, you will be able to use the store's new multi-million-dollar unisex parents' room.

## LET'S PARTY

Babies are a lot of work. It's important, however, that you don't get so wrapped up in the maintenance duties and chores engendered by babies that you forget to actually have some fun with them. It's important that you spend time playing with your baby so that the two of you can get to know each other and build a relationship.

When you do play, give your baby your undivided attention. Some dads seem to think that 'play' means either sitting them in front of the footy on TV or shoving lots of expensive toys in their face. As far as I'm concerned, the best toy is you.

Play can start immediately. What you do depends on the age of your baby. The play should be pitched at the baby's level, not yours. For example, babies are generally hopeless at contact sports. The best suggestions I can make are: be inventive, laugh a lot, don't do anything that scares them, and keep one hand over your testicles at all times.

Here's a list of suggestions:

## Play newborn babies enjoy

- staring at the ceiling;
- having a massage;
- being held;
- looking at your face;
- being sung to; and
- watching you jostle fluffy toys with jingly bells.

## Play older babies enjoy

- chewing (rusks, bananas, mobile phones);
- pulling faces;
- making silly noises;
- rolling around on the floor or bed;
- cuddles;
- dribbling on Dad;
- urinating on Dad;
- vomiting on Dad;
- knee bounces;
- clapping and singing songs;
- peek-a-boo;
- getting raspberries on the stomach;
- being tickled;
- squeaky toys and picture books;
- going for trips in the pram or backpack; and
- and again, massage.

## Play babies don't enjoy

- playing with any toys suitable for babies;
- watching reality television;
- squash;

- computer programming;
- white-water rafting;
- rides on roller-coasters;
- abseiling;
- board games; and
- reading adult fiction without pictures.

Spend time with your baby from Day One. Engage in physical contact. Cuddle it, hold its hands and stroke its hair. Touch and massage are important factors in helping your baby to thrive and feel loved. Find a quiet, warm place and use some baby oil to gently massage your baby's arms and legs, hands and feet, back and stomach.

Sing to your baby. Talk to it. Let it hear your voice. But whatever you do, don't talk or sing to your baby in what you think is their own language. I don't understand why adults persist in doing this. Science has proven that, given the right stimuli, three-month-old babies can not only speak but conduct a decent conversation as well. Unfortunately, most don't because they can't work out what all the adults are saying.

I mean, could you learn to talk if the only thing you ever heard was, 'Bootchie-wootchie-coo-coo. Bubba wanna car-car? Daddy loves his baby bitsy poo-poo. YeeeEEEsssss?'

No wonder babies take years to develop.

Having something of a penchant for music myself, I've always found singing songs to be a most successful and enjoyable form of play. But be warned! Many childhood ditties were composed by people with some serious issues. Have you ever considered, for example, the lyrics of 'Rock-a-Bye-Baby'? This is a song about a baby who has been put in its cradle, not in a nice warm bedroom but in a *treetop*. Aside from the obvious disturbing questions raised by this, the branch then breaks during a storm, and the baby and cradle come crashing through the canopy to the ground. Mmmmm, what a lovely, soothing thought for a baby just as it goes off to sleep.

In addition, many traditional songs are nonsensical to us here in the twenty-first century. For example, what self-respecting father would sing this to a child?

> *Pussy Cat ate the Dumplings,*
> *Shu-o-a, Shu-o-a, Oh Fie.*
> *Poussie, Poussie Boudrons*
> *I got a wee mousie*
> *And nar shan't gar me down*
> *Shu-o-a, Shu-o-a, Oh Fie.*

> *One, two, three, four,*
> *The mutton mutton-bone*
> *'How shall he cut it*
> *Molly Molly-May?'*
> *'With a knife and a wife*
> *And a bale of hay.'*

One alternative is to make up your own songs. I always use established tunes but free-associate my own words. Remember, it doesn't really matter *what* you sing, it's *the way you sing it* that matters.

For example, to the tune of 'Old McDonald Had a Farm':

> *The Dow-Jones just went up five points,*
> *Ee-eye, Ee-eye, oh.*
> *I'll buy more shares in BHP,*
> *Ee-eye, Ee-eye, oh.*
> *There's a fly in the room,*
> *I'm gonna squash it flat,*
> *Then I'm going for a walk*
> *and I really hate this wallpaper,*
> *Hurry up and go to sleep,*
> *Ee-eye, Ee-eye, oh.*

Or this gem, to the tune of 'Amazing Grace':

> *I'm wearing jeans and you are not,*
> *My tax is due today,*
> *The weather is nice,*
> *I like ice-cream,*
> *And my favourite TV show is 'Gilligan's Island'.*

Well, at least I try.

## STEP RIGHT UP!

When Rachael came home, I was ready to play the happy dad just like the ones on the TV commercials. Walks in the park, wrestles on the carpet, throwing her in the air, lots of laughter and fun and tummy-tickling and pulling faces. This was all a great idea, but it did not take me long to discover that newborn babies tend to be fairly sedate.

Some would even say, boring.

Newborn babies, in fact, only perform four basic functions, which they repeat with monotonous regularity:

- They sleep (somewhere around sixteen hours a day; unless you have a baby like The Screamer);
- They cry (a lot, when they're not asleep);
- They drink milk (they want to cry, but their mouth is full); and
- They fill nappies (all the time).

At first I was slightly put out that my backyard camp-outs, fatherly lectures and fruit-juggling would have to wait until Rachael was more developmentally mature. But in the depths of my despair, something wonderful happened.

I'm not doting or sentimental by nature. But one day, soon after the homecoming, Rachael wrapped her minute hand around my index finger and squeezed it like she was milking a cow.

That single little action was a ray of light that made me realise that I was privy to the growth of a little person. At that stage she really did nothing except the usual sleep, cry, drink and crap routine, but I suddenly realised that in the coming months I would see her grow, change and develop. I would see her come to recognise me. I would watch her first steps. I would hear her first words.

And this is exactly what has happened to me three times now.

Like I said, I'm not really doting or sentimental, but with babies, almost every day brings something new. It really is quite thrilling to participate in the life and growth of your baby. But don't expect too much at once. Most new parents spend a lot of time staring at their babies, cameras poised, waiting for the next important developmental milestone to occur. And as soon as the baby even moves, they take a photo and email it to all their friends. Then when their one-year-old beats the keys of a piano with clenched fists they will scream, 'Did you hear that? Did you hear that? Beethoven's *Fifth*!! Child prodigy!!'

I even fell into the trap. One day, Rachael was lying on her stomach during her third month. Her leg went into a spasm and kicked out – the way babies' legs do – and she nudged forward an inch.

The next day I told some of my work colleagues that Rachael could crawl even though she was only two months old. They looked at me with the tolerant and knowing smiles of parental experience. Their faces had *new father with ridiculously high expectations* written all over them.

Growing up is a slow and laborious process. Your baby won't do everything overnight. But then again, that's part of the fun.

So what exactly can you expect, and when? Well, here's a rough guide to the developmental stages of babies. Remember, though, that I'm not a medical doctor or a child psychologist or anything like that. The following list is less the result of any serious empirical analysis and more the result of watching babies down at the local playgroup.

At zero months, you can expect your baby to:

- cry, drink, vomit, crap, sleep (repeat);
- be a blob on the carpet; and
- get fluffy toys and bibs from your friends.

At three months, you can expect your baby to:

- smile;
- shake a rattle;
- play with its hands;
- start to lift its head; and
- be responsive to you.

At six months, you can expect your baby to:

- start getting teeth;
- bite you with its teeth;
- produce 'teething nappies' (the worst you'll ever experience);
- use hands to pick up disgusting objects;
- use hands to put disgusting objects into mouth;
- eat foods other than breastmilk;
- gurgle and sing to itself; and
- sit up for a few seconds without bashing its head on the floor.

At nine months, you can expect your baby to:

- sit up;
- stand up holding onto things;
- crawl; and
- never shut up.

At twelve months, you can expect your baby to:

- recognise its name;
- eat finger food;

- remove own nappy and eat anything it finds within;
- walk with the assistance of a trolley;
- stumble from trolley and smack head into wall;
- bite you a lot; and
- throw tantrums in public places.

At fifteen months, you can expect your baby to:

- start on basic words (that is, if you count 'Dog! Dog!' as speaking);
- stumble dangerously around at high speeds;
- eat small serves of what you eat;
- have favourite toys or books;
- get into places where it shouldn't be;
- nod to indicate *yes* and *no*, and wave goodbye; and
- own shoes that are more expensive than yours.

At eighteen months, you can expect your baby to:

- point at things it wants;
- demand to have your attention all the time;
- understand basic commands, like 'No!' and 'Fetch!';
- break something very valuable;
- contract a mystery illness which will make you very worried;
- take half an hour to dress; and
- flush valuable items down the toilet.

At twenty-four months, you can expect your baby to:

- use a 'big' toilet, with some assistance;
- use a spoon;
- play by itself;
- have a basic vocabulary and primitive sentence construction; and
- have a junk-food addiction.

At thirty months, you can expect your baby to:

- ask you unanswerable questions like
  *Where is the world?*
  *Why is red?*
  *Why aren't I a tree?*;
- ride a pedal tricycle; and
- know the jingle from every irritating commercial on TV.

At thirty-six months, you can expect your baby to:

- read a couple of words;
- stumble into your bedroom every night;
- operate complicated home-entertainment-unit remote controls;
- know what foods it dislikes; and
- strike up conversations with strangers at the supermarket, based on phrases such as
  *You're fat!*
  *Where's your hair?*
  *Do you have a penis? My Dad does.*

At 108 months, you can expect your baby to:

- start asking for more pocket money;
- want a horse or drum kit for Christmas;
- want every show-bag at the Easter Show; and
- come out with its first swear words.

At 144 months, you can expect your baby to:

- want to get its ears pierced;
- have its own mobile phone;
- have its mobile phone disconnected because it spent over $500 on calls that month; and
- be able to run faster than you.

At 180 months, you can expect your baby to:

- bring home its first love, whom you won't like at all;
- want to get its navel/eyebrow/nose pierced;
- spend hours in the bathroom; and
- triple your phone bill.

At 216 months, you can expect your baby to:

- go to an R-rated film;
- come home at 2 am and get grounded for ten years;
- drink alcohol legally; and
- want to borrow your car.

At 252 months, you can expect your baby to:

- be earning more than you; and
- have a baby.

Yep, as they get older it just gets better. This way, like a fine wine, you enjoy it more.

By the way, kids never perform any of their new feats in front of strangers. They are like Mr Ed, the talking horse. Mr Ed would chat away to Wilbur all day, but the moment someone else entered the stable he would just be an ordinary horse again.

Your baby may be able to clap hands or play peek-a-boo. It might be able to stand on its head or discuss environmental issues in a second language. It might be able to sing opera or perform complex mathematical functions while tap-dancing. But the moment guests arrive at your place, it will revert to being a baby. You will ask it to do things and it will stare at you dumbly and your friends will think you're an idiot.

So when you have guests, never say, 'Baby David ... come here ... yes, yes ... come on, that's the boy! Tell Aunty Sue the square root of nine.'

The baby will look at you and will invariably respond with, 'DOG!'

'C'mon, you know the answer ... *please*,' you will plead.

'SNOT!'

And be assured that the moment Aunty Sue steps out the door, the baby will mumble, 'Three.'

## SECURE THE HOUSE

Once things have settled down a bit in your home and you and your wife are getting used to the idea of living with a baby, there are some further changes you'll need to make around the place.

As I mentioned earlier, newborns don't move around much by themselves. With the exception of change-tables, they basically lie wherever you leave them, like a turtle on its back. Therefore they don't really have much of an impact on the way your place is set out. However, in the coming months your baby will learn to crawl. Some babies have a top speed that would impress a cheetah in hot pursuit of a wildebeest. You put them down, blink ... and all you can see is a vapour trail of nappy fumes as they tear off down the corridor.

The problem is that this new-found mobility gives your baby access to all sorts of wonderful dangers around the home. Babies are naturally inquisitive – but have no concept of danger whatsoever. So it's really important that you baby-proof your home.

Here are some ideas:

- Stairs, windows, balconies, swimming pools, fishtanks and fishponds should be secured. Fences, railings and banisters should have vertical slats inserted between the main beams to prevent small bodies from squeezing through or climbing over. You should also put gates at the head and foot of staircases to prevent any unsupervised acrobatics from occurring.

- Every ground-level power-point should be fitted with plastic plug to prevent infant electricians from experimenting with death. Also make sure that all double adaptors and power-boards are secure and out of reach. Make sure your place has an electrical safety switch which cuts the power supply in some incredible fraction of a second in the event of the baby wedging a fork into a power-point or pulling a badly placed hairdryer into its bath. (Then again, if you are doing your job, there shouldn't be a hairdryer there anyway.) Our place is old, but it didn't cost much to get a switch supplied and fitted. Baby aside, our safety switch has saved my life on several occasions. (I didn't know the toaster was plugged in. Honest.) This is an absolutely essential investment.

- All dangerous household products and objects (cleaning fluids, sprays, powders, medicines, knives, Michael Jackson DVDs, etc.) should be put in top drawers or locked cupboards. This is particularly the case in the kitchen, bathroom and laundry. Every week in Australia, about fifty kids end up in hospital because they've guzzled something they shouldn't have. There are a range of easy-to-install devices available from your local hardware store to prevent this from happening, ranging from plastic hooks to an electrified chain with a six-digit computerised combination lock. Such a device will keep your baby out for about two or three days.

  Also check that cockroach baits and mousetraps are inaccessible, and remember that kids can reach up higher than their heads. I learnt this the hard way, when Rachael cleaned her teeth one morning with a disposable razor which I'd assumed was 'out of reach'.

- If there is water around, *do not take your eyes off your baby*. If the phone rings during bath-time, take the baby with you or let the damn thing ring out. Always keep the lids on nappy buckets and put them in an inaccessible room. When you've finished using the nappy buckets, empty them and turn them upside-down.

- Secure freestanding shelves, drawers or cupboards. Babies are good at climbing, but their King Kong-like behaviour may lead to disaster if their weight is enough to topple a piece of furniture.

- Make sure that there are no saucepan handles sticking out from the stove, or power leads dangling down from anywhere. To a baby, a dangling cable is an inviting vine on which they will inevitably try to swing like Tarzan. The problem is that it is probably attached to an iron or toaster or kettle. You can imagine the rest.

- Guard all fires, including heaters and stoves. If you can, keep your baby dressed in natural fibres such as cotton or wool, which are more fire-resistant than manufactured materials. Also, keep matches well away from babies. If they don't light them, they'll certainly eat them or stick them up their nose.

- Don't leave plastic bags lying around, and don't let your baby put buttons, nuts, coins, the eyes of fluffy toys and so on into their mouths. They may choke.

- Ensure there are no Venetian blind strings or curtain cords near the baby's cot or play areas. These may get tangled around its neck.

- Make sure that all things you value – especially electrical items – are suspended from the ceiling by cables or else are only accessible by ladder. If you've ever seen the damage a bowl of spaghetti can do to a DVD player, you'll know what I'm talking about.

- If your place has a low ceiling fan, be very, very careful. It's easy to forget they are up there spinning away, and when Uncle Frank comes to visit and decides to play spaceships with Baby Jessica ... well, you can imagine the rest.

Even after you've done all these things and a couple of others that you thought up along the way, there is one more thing that you must do. It sounds a bit weird, but it's the most effective way of finding out how safe your home actually is. Here's how it works.

First, get down on your hands and knees and pretend that you are an inquisitive baby.

Second, crawl around from room to room, seeing how much damage you can do to the nice things within your reach. See if you can find some computer disks to chew or some fragile ornaments to smash.

Third, crawl around from room to room, seeing how much damage you can do to *yourself*. Try to find great heights to leap off and nasty things to stick in your mouth. You will be surprised at what you discover.

There's one other thing that you must remember at all times. It doesn't really apply to baby-proofing your home – unless you live in a glasshouse, that is – but it's vitally important anyway.

A newborn's skin is about one thousand times more sensitive than your leathery hide. This is not helped by the depletion of the ozone layer and Australia's naturally sunny climate. A baby can burn easily, even on a cloudy day. So never put your baby out for a sunbake. (In fact, never put *anyone* out for a sunbake.) This particularly applies to outdoor outings such as to the beach. Avoid exposure to the sun, especially in the middle of the day, and always ensure your baby is wearing a sunscreen with a sun protection factor (SPF) of 30+, plus a hat and sun shirt. You could even get a little pair of wrap-around shades. Also, put a tea towel or shade-screen in your car window to stop the sun frying them in their capsule. Make sure, though, that you put the towel on a *side* window, not the *front* window. This will maintain your driving visibility.

## OF CATS AND DOGS

Some friends of mine recently had a dilemma. They had two big dogs whom they had raised from pups. These dogs had been the sole guardians and masters of their house for years and were regarded and treated almost like children.

But that had to change, because one day my friends had a baby. Some of the canine privileges obviously had to go. So while mother and baby were resting in hospital before the home-coming, the brilliant father thought up a grand scheme to desensitise the dogs to the baby.

I remember sitting in their lounge room days before the big return. This mate of mine sat the dogs down in front of him and produced from a plastic bag a wad of used nappies that he had brought from the hospital. He rubbed the dogs' faces in them and said the baby's name over and over: '*Anna, Anna, Anna ...*'

Something didn't seem quite right. The dogs' eyes were glistening a little too brightly for my liking. All I could think of was an old black and white movie I had seen where a British lord threw his bloodthirsty hounds a jumper belonging to an escaped convict. They sniffed and growled at it and then galloped off across the moors to hunt him down and rip him to pieces.

*pets can get jealous ...*

Maybe it wasn't really such a good idea after all.

Some people are dog people. Some people are cat people. Some are hairy-nosed aardvark people. I'm not much of a pet person. I had a dog when I was a kid, but I had to feed it and that meant opening tins of dog food, which scarred me for life. I vowed I'd never have a pet when I got older. I did end up getting some guinea pigs for the girls, but they were sad, pathetic, timid creatures that died of fright in a thunderstorm.

If you *do* have a pet, you need to think through the implications of bringing a new member of the family into your house.

The main problem is that pets can get jealous. A big dog could eat a baby before you could blink, particularly if they are called Killer and wear a studded collar. Cats have been known to attack newborns by sticking their tail into the baby's mouth until it gets a furball. (The baby that is, not the cat.) Even axolotls have been known to try to slime babies to death. I shouldn't even need to mention boa constrictors.

As far as I can make out, there are only a few pets you can keep when you have a new baby in your house. Budgies are stuck in a cage, so they can't fly over and rip your baby's throat out with their steely talons. Guinea pigs are just plain stupid. If you've got fish, they're probably OK. They aren't dangerous, unless your baby tries to eat one. And then you've got the risk of drowning. Again, make sure the fishtank is inaccessible.

Come to think of it, horses are probably OK too, as long as you don't let them into the nursery.

## REMEMBERING TO BE A COUPLE

You and your wife used to be a couple. Now you're a family.

You used to be a pair. Now you're a trio.

You used to be tennis partners. Now you're almost a basketball team.

The point is this. Having a baby in the house changes your relationship with your wife. This is because you don't spend as much time together as you used to. You used to go out to dinner and go for walks and see movies and talk intimately and all those other things that couples do. You used to have lots of time to invest in the maintenance and development of your relationship.

But that was before the baby. Sure, there are lots of things you can still do, but it certainly won't be as easy anymore. The threat to your relationship is reflected in the words of some old famous poet I studied at school: 'No time. No time. Too much to do.' The baby needs to be fed. The shopping needs to be done. The baby needs to be changed. The nappies need to be put on the line. The baby needs to be sung to sleep. The house needs a vacuum. The baby needs a bath. The dinner has to be cooked. The washing up hasn't been done in days.

The problem is that you and your wife can end up running around doing baby and house-type maintenance duties and then all of a sudden you wake up one morning and wonder who the strange person next to you in your bed is. The face seems oddly familiar ... Oh, that's right ... you're married to her!

If you're not careful, your relationship with your wife can go out the window. I've heard of parents who, after many years, when their kids leave home, sadly realise that they don't really know each other anymore. They were so busy being parents that they forgot to be husband and wife.

This is tragic.

The message is, *don't forget to be a good husband*.

Don't neglect your wife.

You must both make a deliberate attempt to spend some time alone together – even if it is only a few desperately grabbed moments. Have a cup of tea together. Try to have a meal with just the two of you. Lie in bed for ten minutes before you get up. A little way down the track you can extend this. You might be able to catch a movie or have a hit of tennis or a walk or swim.

Your relationship with your wife is really important. Don't forget it. And don't assume that Mother's Day is the only day of the year she gets treated to something special. Mother's Day is a disgusting concept promoted by retail outlets wanting to make a quick buck. Forget chocolates and roses. The best way to show your appreciation is by your words and actions. Give your wife love offerings like a cooked dinner or a clean bathroom floor. Mind the baby while she goes out and does whatever it is she wants to do. Tell her you love her and that you want to do that thing with the cooking oil and the lamp-shade.

## EVEN MORE ON SEX

Many new fathers find that sex is relegated to that part of their brain clearly labelled 'distant memory'. According to some statistics, nearly all mothers and 50 per cent of fathers are less interested in sex during the post-birth period.

The problem, though, is that nothing can shatter a husband's ego like a wife uninterested in sex. It's easy therefore to feel a little resentful that things aren't what they used to be. You can resent the baby, because if it wasn't for its crying, crying, crying all the time, your sex life would be great, great, great. You can become jealous of all the attention lavished upon your baby by your wife – attention that used to be lavished upon you.

But given that mums are usually exhausted from working twenty-four hours a day, it's actually perfectly understandable that your wife might not be as interested in you as she used to be. The last thing she feels like is another physically and emotionally demanding marathon in the cot. She needs sleep.

A friend once told me a horror story about 'a friend of a friend' of theirs who had just had her first child. She was sharing her hospital room in the maternity ward with another woman. According to this friend of a friend, the husband of this other woman came into the room soon after her labour and 'had his way' with her.

Stuff like this makes my skin crawl. Given that this happened to a woman acquainted to a friend of a friend of a friend, I suspect it is an urban myth, up there with the likes of the cat in the microwave, the hitchhiking ghost, the murderer on the roof of the car and the genuine department-store sale.

If, on the other hand, there really are men like this in the world, it makes me embarrassed to be called a male. The guy obviously had a sloping forehead and scars on his knuckles from where they scraped along the ground. This type of behaviour is Neanderthal and completely inexcusable.

Once you see what happens to your wife's body in childbirth, particularly if a caesarean or episiotomy were involved, I'm sure you will understand why your wife would rather be left alone than mauled by you. Her postnatal body weight distribution and maternity bra probably don't help make her feel like Aphrodite, anyway. Rumour also has it that cracked nipples are not conducive to sensual arousal. If you can't comprehend this, give your pectorals a brisk rub with a sheet of sandpaper and then see how raunchy you feel.

When you start playing the role of the active dad and get into night-settling and nappy-changing and baby-bathing, you'll probably get a small inkling of why she's not so interested in sex. But for the moment, let's go back to the anecdote about the umbrella and your penis. Meditate on this for a while. Imagine stretching your penis so far that you can scratch your nose with it. Imagine unmentionable acts with your scrotum and an insinkerator. Imagine urinating a grapefruit. I'm sure you wouldn't feel like a heavy session of intense passion after that. And you wouldn't appreciate your wife giving you the 'nudge-nudge, wink-wink' treatment, either.

In this regard, then, let your wife call the shots regarding your mutual re-entry (I'm sorry, I couldn't help it) into the world of love-making.

Of course, it's not just your wife's recovery from the physical trauma of labour and birth that inhibits your sex life. It's also the fact that you are both perpetually exhausted and are lucky if you have a moment to yourselves. It's also a little-known fact that newborn babies have a psychic link with their mothers, which means they can detect any sexual arousal or activity within a 100-metre radius. This will immediately trigger a screaming response just at 'the critical moment' – if you know what I mean.

## WHEN YOU'RE OUT OF YOUR DEPTH

No one expects either you or your wife to be an instantaneous parental expert. Even if you have read widely and spoken to parental pioneers, there will still be times when you feel out of your depth and unsure if things are going as they should.

Your baby may not sleep well. It might look pale, or it might cough all the time. It may cry constantly without apparent reason. It might not go on the breast very well. Blotches or marks may appear on its skin.

Sometimes, you need practical advice or assistance. Sometimes, however, people want to give you advice even when you don't want it or need it. Suddenly everyone is an expert and knows exactly how to solve your paternal problems.

If anyone without kids of their own gives you advice, disregard it totally. They don't know what they're talking about. If they are persistent, ask them to change your baby's nappy. That'll shut them up.

If any strangers in the supermarket try to give you advice, pretend you don't speak English.

Family is a little different. After all, your parents brought you up and you turned out OK. But remember too that it was your mum who used to put butter on your burns when you were a kid, and your dad still calls your very expensive home-entertainment unit a *wireless*.

My grandmother always seems full of good ideas – but how much can I trust a woman who thinks tripe on toast for breakfast is a pretty good idea?

Hospitals, early childhood and community health centres and your doctor are good starting points for help. In addition, there are a number of organisations that exist to help novice parents particularly in relation to getting help in setting up sleeping routines, such as Tresillian and Karitane in New South Wales and the Queen Elizabeth Centre and Tweddle Baby Hospital in Victoria.

Don't hesitate in seeking advice from one of these places. Many people do. Establishing good sleeping patterns is really important, but it can be difficult and frustrating. It might be that you need an answer over the phone, or it might be that mother and baby need to spend a few nights in 'sleep school' to get them into a better sleeping and feeding routine. We were having a few problems with Rachael's nocturnal crying, so Meredith stayed at a Tresillian centre for a few days and found it to be excellent. The mothercraft nurses encouraged Meredith and assured her she was doing the right thing. They also gave her practical advice and demonstrated coping mechanisms. It made a big difference.

Don't be afraid to get help!

## THE PARENTING SECRET

Earlier in the book, I quoted the lines from the Ron Howard film *Parenthood*:

> *'You know ... you need a licence to buy a dog or drive a car. Hell, you need a licence to catch a fish. But they'll let any ... asshole be a father.'*

It is also with this quote that I will close this book.

It took me four years at university to become a qualified secondary school teacher. Four years of lectures, seminars and tutorials. Four years of burning the midnight oil, drinking industrial-strength coffee and writing impossibly long essays and papers. Four years researching and analysing expert opinions in gigantic leather-bound volumes found in the darkest recesses of a labyrinthine library.

But it was all worth it. At the end of the four years I was ready to set the educational world on fire. I knew all there was to be known. I was an expert in school policy, child psychology, curriculum development, time management and literary analysis. I had done the work and was ready to assume my God-given role in life: *superteacher*.

With a brand-new testamur under my arm, I sailed out of university into a job in an independent school. At the end of a lengthy summer holiday, I turned up for my first day of work sporting a post-university haircut and a new suit. My head was held high, because my final grade at university had been a high distinction. I knew this would demand instant respect in the staffroom and guarantee me obedience and honour from the student body for the rest of my life. I was instantly recognisable as an expert. It was all plain-sailing from here. Easy.

Then I met Graham.

Graham was my department head, a bloke who looked like he forgot to get out of his clothes before he threw them into the dryer for a good tumble. I'll never forget our first meeting. He sat me down in his small office and, with a fair whack of theatrical flair, said, 'Welcome to the real world. You've spent four years with your head up in the clouds in some educational ivory tower. Now it's time to come down to Earth. Forget most of the stuff you learnt at uni. It's crap. Get into the classroom, keep 'em under control, teach 'em something and get out alive. That's it. Any questions?'

I was shocked, to say the least. Hadn't this man seen my curriculum vitae? Didn't he know who I was? Didn't he know that I had read all the books and had sat at the feet of the great academic masters? I'd got a high distinction, for heaven's sake! But before I could voice an objection, he was on his feet and out the door. With a glance back over his shoulder, he chipped in, 'You're going to learn more this week about being a teacher than you did in four years of having your head stuck in books. Have a nice day.'

He was right. At the end of that first week, I realised that I really knew little about teaching. I was a humbled amateur and each night as I crawled exhausted into bed I would think, *Why didn't anybody tell me about this? Why wasn't I warned?* I was an expert on theory, but practice – that would have to come in time.

A few years later, I became a father. I had read all the books, been to all the classes, and surfed the websites. I knew all the theories and was ready to assume my other God-given role in life: *superfather*. And exactly the same thing happened. I learnt more in that first week after Rachael's birth than I did in nine months of preparation.

So, you can read all the books and magazines on parenting in the local library. You can watch every film on childbirth ever made. You can ask questions of medical staff until their ears fall off. You can study all the current theories and attend birth classes until you're an expert. In fact, it is your responsibility to do these things.

But it will still be 'academic'. It will still be head-knowledge.

And now that you've almost finished this tome, I'll let you in on a little secret. Are you ready? It's printed in bold so you can't miss it. OK, here it is:

**Nothing can really prepare you for becoming a father.**

I hope you're not disappointed, but I had to put this earth-shattering statement at the end of the last chapter, otherwise you might not have read the book.

Until you experience fatherhood in all its rewarding and painful glory, you can't really know what it's like in the 3-D, Dolby surround sense of the word. You have to *live it* to get the full sensation. Only when you feel the kick of your unborn child do you feel the thrill of expectation. Only when you see your wife give birth do you really understand how painful it is. Only when you hear crying at 3 am do you know what it is to be tired and cranky. Only when you change a nappy for the first time do you know the true meaning of nausea. Only when your baby says 'I lub oo, dabbee' when you tuck them in at night do you feel that bursting excitement and pride of fatherhood.

But that's OK.

You are not alone. Every dad who ever lived was in your shoes once too. They were as nervous and uncertain and excited as you are. And the human race seems to have gotten on just fine.

The whole idea is that dadhood is a *learning process*. It's on-the-job training of the most important kind. And you'd better get used to it, because before you know it, your wife will be pregnant again. (And again.) Just when you think you're in the home straight, you'll be back at GO without even collecting the two hundred dollars.

# EPILOGUE

If I were to leave you with a message as you face the months ahead – at whatever stage you are at – it would be this:

Don't give up.

Sometimes things don't go the way you plan.

Being a dad is not always great and wonderful times. It's not always holding hands and piggy-back rides and 'I love you Dad'. There are busy times, rotten times, tired times, times when you are irritated and feel lousy.

The important thing is not that you become the perfect father, because there is no such thing. The important thing is that when things don't look so good – when things go wrong, when you make mistakes – that you try again.

It took me quite a while to learn this. My dad tried to warn me, but I didn't listen.

He said that fatherhood was like riding a bicycle. I didn't understand at first. Riding a bicycle is about travelling very fast, wearing tight lycra and grazing your knees. Fatherhood, on the other hand, is about changing dirty nappies and not getting a good night's sleep anymore.

Not very similar if you ask me.

But there was a message in the heart of old Dad's metaphor. You don't learn to ride a bike by studying the principles of circular motion, gear ratios and muscle development. In reality you get on the bike, you pedal hard, you fall off and then you get on again and repeat the process until the 'you fall off' bit doesn't happen with such frightening regularity anymore.

Just like fatherhood.

You have to keep going. You have to keep trying. You have to keep getting back up on the bike.

So you're now the fully-fledged father of a real live baby. You have navigated the pregnancy, survived the labour and stumbled through life at home with a newborn person. Soon you will get used to this new life and you will start to feel comfortable and in control again. You will find your feet and look back and wonder what all the fuss was about in the first place.

To an extent, this is an appropriate feeling to have. But don't be deceived. Don't start relaxing. Pretty soon, your baby is going to learn to walk and talk.

Soon your baby will turn into ... *a toddler*.

That's when hell really breaks loose. Because if you thought living with a baby was hard, you ain't seen nothin' yet.

But you can read about that in the sequel I wrote to this book: *Dads, Toddlers and the Chicken Dance*.

So to you, my paternal comrades, I offer my congratulations on being given the awesome responsibility and tremendous privilege of being a father. Although it might not be obvious right now, this is the most important thing you are going to do in your life. I hope you embrace it in all its richness and wonder. Savour the golden times, struggle through the frustrating times, and work hard at it.

I hope in some small way this book has given you a glimpse of the pain, frustration, pleasure, joy and even comedy of dadhood. I hope it has helped you prepare for your own journey as a dad.

I used to think that this journey down the parental road was a pretty straight one. You walked down it for a while until you arrived at your destination – parental perfection. I've since come to realise that this road is in fact a windy and complex maze. Sometimes I don't seem to be getting anywhere. And the further I travel through this maze, the more I realise that there is in fact no destination. There is no exit. I'll never get to a point where I stop being a parent. I'll be journeying until the day I die. Until then, I'll plough ahead, keeping one eye to the front and the other on the lookout for puddles.

Occasionally I look back on where I've come from and realise that parenting has brought me a deep sense of satisfaction and contentment. It has redefined who I am. And although I suspect parenting just gets harder from here on, I'm really, *really* looking forward to the years ahead.

I hope you are too.

Good luck on your journey … Dad.

# GLOSSARY

This is not an extensive glossary. It just contains a whole lot of words that I know.

**Aaarrgghh no it can't possibly be true it must be a nightmare I'm going to vomit … uurrgghblecchpphhilhh** The words often spoken by dads changing their first teething nappy.

**after birth** (i) The time immediately following the birth of the baby; (ii) All the stuff that comes out of the mother after the baby is born.

**after pains** The pain you feel after the birth when the bills start arriving.

**aglet** The plastic covering on the end of a shoelace.

**Alfa Romeo** The car driven by your doctor.

**amniocentesis** The extraction and testing of the amniotic fluid for abnormalities in the foetus.

**amniotic fluid** Fluid inside the bag that the baby grows up inside.

**amniotic inversion** This is nothing, really. I just made it up.

**amniotic sac** The bag that the baby grows up inside.

**amniotomy** Using a hook to rupture the amniotic sac.

**anaesthetic** Thing which helps you cope with pain. Often used by mothers during labour (injections or gas) and fathers getting used to a newborn (bourbon or beer).

*Antipericatametaanaparcircumvolutiorectumgustpoops of the Coprofied* The title of a book on a shelf in the library in the classic work *Gargantua and Pantagruel* by Francois Rabelais.

**Apgar test** (i) Test used to upgrade a level within the Swedish Civil Service; named after Thor *Apgar,* Swedish prime minister and mountain climber; (ii) Used after birth to rate the newborn's heart-rate, breathing, skin and muscle tone, reflexes and sense of humour.

**Audi** The car driven by your obstetrician's spouse.

**augmentation** Making the labour go faster.

**baby** The technical name given to your child after it's finished being a foetus.

**Beta hCG** (human chorionic gonadotrophin) A nasty hormone.

**beta max** Less popular although technically superior video recorder.

**bilirubin** (i) The pigment which builds up in the bloodstream, giving jaundiced babies their telltale colour; (ii) I know you're not going to believe this, but I actually went to primary school with a kid called Billy Ruben. I swear it's true. Kind of.

**birth** When the baby comes out of the mother.

**Birth Canal** (i) Salt-water inlet located approximately fifty kilometres south of the Suez Canal; (ii) The passage that the baby has to navigate to get out of the mother.

**blues** (i) Soulful music portraying a depressed character and morbid world-view; (ii) Sadness felt during postnatal period largely attributed to hormonal changes in the mother's body; (iii) Hues between green and violet.

**BMW** The car driven by your obstetrician.

**Bond** British super-spy rated with a 00 licence to kill. First name: James.

**bonding** What happens when you pick your baby up with hands covered in super glue.

**boozeesukka** What babies do to get milk out of their mothers.

**bottle** Container used for formula transfer to baby.

**bouncer** (i) Gorilla-like male who stands outside nightclubs and decides whether you're trendy enough to get in; (ii) A device for baby bouncing.

**Braxton Hicks** Irritating and extremely inconveniencing false labour contractions. (*See also* Corporal Hicks.)

**breast** (i) The bit my family always fight over when we have roast chicken for dinner; (ii) One of the two outermost points on your wife's front bit, usually impressively swollen to dirigible size by the time of birth.

**breast feeding** (i) When whoever was successful in the fight we have when my family has roast chicken for dinner eats their meal; (ii) When the baby drinks from its mother.

**breast pump** Gigantic device which looks like the bug-catcher you got for your seventh birthday. It makes *schloop, schlurp* noises and sucks breast milk out.

**breech birth** When the baby is born bum-first.

**Caesar, Julius** Roman statesman and general, 100–44 BC.

**Caesar Romero** Played *The Cisco Kid* and the original Joker from *Batman.*

**caesar salad** A tasty mix of cos lettuce, croutons, bacon, anchovies, egg, parmesan cheese, oil and vinegar.

**caesarean section** (i) The quarter of Rome where Caesar's supporters lived; (ii) The surgical removal of stubborn unborns.

**caretonoids** I have no idea what these are.

**cervix** The bottom of the uterus. Something akin to the plughole.

**chromosomes** Microscopic thread-like structures which contain thousands of genes. Each cell has twenty-three chromosomes. (*See also* X chromosome and Y chromosome.)

**circumcision** Cutting off the squidgy bit on the end of the penis. Not to be confused with castration or circumlocution.

**colic** A condition during which babies scream and scream and yell and wail and you go psycho-bananas trying to cope with it.

**colostrum** A rich breast secretion, jam-packed full of proteins, antibodies and other nourishing stuff, which flows for a few days after birth before the milk kicks in.

**conception** When the fertilised egg buries itself in the uterus.

**condominium** (i) American block of flats; (ii) The smallest size of a rubber contraceptive. The other sizes are condomediocre and condomammoth.

**contraceptive** Well it's too late now, isn't it?

**Corporal Hicks** The hero of the movie *Aliens.* (*See also* Braxton Hicks.)

**crowning** (i) When a monarch receives their symbolic headpiece of power; (ii) When the baby's head appears on the way out.

**delivery** When somebody brings you something, such as a pizza. Or a baby.

**depression** A state of sadness or moodiness encountered by parents. For mothers, it occurs usually after the birth. For fathers, it is when they realise that babies are really expensive, cause sleep deprivation and ruin their social and sex lives.

**dilation** The process of being made wider. For example, the pupils of your eyes when you enter a dark room, or the cervix when it realises that the baby is about to try to pass through it.

**duff** (i) The decaying organic matter on the forest floor; (ii) The brand of beer favoured by Homer Simpson; (iii) The place your wife went up to, to get pregnant.

**eight-thirty pm** The universally acknowledged time for parents to leave parties.

**embryo** Another name for your child; technically from implantation until about the twelfth week of pregnancy.

**endorphins** The body's natural opiates.

**enema** Totally excellent activity for the whole family in which you get a little squirt of fluid up the old recto and everything hiding in your lower bowel comes out with great haste and enthusiasm. This is used sometimes for women in labour as part of the service. However, in California you can get one done just for fun.

**engaged** (i) When you promise to marry your girlfriend; (ii) When the baby gets ready for birth during the last month of pregnancy by turning into the *eject position*.

**engorgement** This is when the mother's breasts go overboard on the milk production and get bigger and bigger and sorer and sorer. If left untreated, they can explode and cause a lot of damage.

**epidural block** (i) The anaesthetic procedure of wasting the entire lower half of a woman by injecting stuff into her lower spine; (ii) Another name for part of the hospital, like the Admin. Block or Respite Block.

**episiotomy** A surgical cut in the perineum to make it bigger so the baby can get out. This is done to prevent or impede tearing.

**Fallopian tubes** The tunnels between the ovaries and the uterus where fertilisation takes place.

**fertilisation** When the sperm and the ovum get together. This is the very first step in the production of human life.

**flaccid** Soft and drooping.

**floccinaucinihilipipification** The habit of estimating something as worthless.

**foetal distress** When complications arise during birth causing a shortage of oxygen to the baby; i.e., when the umbilical cord gets tangled or pinched.

**foetal distress flare** A bright red emergency light which shoots out of the vagina and into the delivery suite to let everyone know that problems are developing.

**foetus** The name of your baby after the period when it is an embryo; technically from after the twelfth week of pregnancy until birth.

**fontanelle** (i) The soft spots on the foetus' or newborn's head where the skull has yet to join together; (ii) A region of Italy known for its cheese, mushroom and pepper sauce. Next time you're in an Italian restaurant, ask for *Fontanelle Ravioli* or *Fettuccine Fontanelle*.

**forceps** Gigantic baby-grabbing pliers.

**foreskin** The squidgy bit on the end of your penis, but if you are of my generation (i.e. born in the Sixties), you probably don't have one so don't bother looking. (*See also* circumcision.)

**Gamma Globulin** When the travellers in the classic series 'Lost in Space' get thrown off-course because of the malevolent but ultimately likeable Dr Zachary Smith, they miss Alpha Centauri and crash-land on Planet EV 36, also known as Planet Gamma Globulin, where they encounter a horrific giant Cyclops which throws rocks at their spacecraft.

**genes** (i) Expensive denim work-pants with designer labels and French names; (ii) Little, really really microscopically tiny things that carry genetic information within cells.

**getchadamhanzoff!** Common maternal expression yelled at inconsiderate groping husbands.

**glossary** Pathetic and see-through attempt to beef out a book by slapping another couple of irrelevant pages on the end.

**gynaecologist** A doctor of woman's things.

**harp** The metal hoop that supports a lampshade.

**hepaticocholecystostcholecystenterostomy** The surgical formation of a passage between the gall bladder and the hepatic duct.

**hormones** Chemicals in the bloodstream that act as messengers to activate specific organs in the body to some type of response. During pregnancy, women have a lot of these floating around. (Chemicals that is, not organs.)

**hospital** A place with doctors and nurses where you go when you're sick … but that's not important right now.

**immunisation** The process whereby you protect your child from getting deadly diseases.

**implantation** This is when the sperm-ovum blobby thing picks out a cosy spot in the uterine wall to call home.

**incubator** A sealed crib used for monitoring newborns.

**induction** (i) When American presidents are officially put into office. This is usually accompanied by tears, moving words ripped off from JFK, appearances by Michael Jackson and saxophone-playing; (ii) The artificial triggering of labour.

**intravenous drip** A slow feed line of fluid from a bag into the vein by way of a catheter.

**ixoye** I'm not sure what this means. I think it's Greek or something historical like that.

**Jaguar** Your obstetrician's other car.

**jaundice** A common newborn thing where the baby's liver doesn't do something or other and something else happens and then the baby turns yellow.

**khaki** A word which all Americans find difficult to pronounce correctly.

**knackers** Slang term for dangly male bits which started this whole dad thing in the first place.

**labour** (i) The hard work experienced by a woman in getting the baby out of her; (ii) One of the main political parties in Australia, increasingly similar to the Liberal Party.

**lanugo** A covering of body hair at birth, usually accompanied by the comment, 'Oh look, it's a carpet!'

**let down** (i) When a woman's milk drops into her breasts; (ii) The feeling you get when your wife goes out to get a DVD and comes back with *Sleepless in Seattle*.

**lopadotemachoselachogaleokranioleipsanodrimhypotrimmatosilphiopar aomelitokatakechymenokichlepikosyphophattoperisteralektryonoptek ephalliokigklopeleiolagoiosiraiobaphetraganopterygonn** The English translation of a Greek word meaning: 'A goulash composed of all the leftovers from the meals of the last two weeks'.

**Mars** The place where your wife would rather be than on the delivery couch.

**mastitis** Painful breast problem where breasts get lumpy and as sore as testicles that have just been trodden on by a troupe of Morris dancers.

**meconium** The technical name given to a baby's first bowel movements. In some Third World nations it is used to surface roads. Don't let it come into contact with bare skin.

**memory** The place in your brain under which you should file 'sex'.

**Mercedes Benz** The car your obstetrician drives when they're sick of the Jaguar.

**midhusband** There's no such thing, but this is a perfect example of how the degenderisation of our language only works one way. (*See also* midwife.)

**midwife** A nurse who specialises in childbirth.

**milk** Nutritious stuff that comes out of cows and women.

**morning sickness** When a woman feels so gross and nauseous during pregnancy that she wishes she were rather watching re-runs of 'Oprah'.

**mucus** Nasal discharge.

**nappy** Crap catcher.

**nausea gravidarum** Morning sickness.

**navel** Lumpy thing on the lower stomach.

**nipples** Two lumpy things on the end of the breasts.

**nitrous oxide gas** Anaesthetic also referred to as *laughing gas,* although I'm not sure why anyone would want to laugh during childbirth.

**obstetrician** A specialist doctor who delivers babies and drives an expensive car.

**oestrogen** A hormone produced in large quantities during pregnancy.

**osseocarnisanguineoviscericartilagininervomedullary** A term detailing the structure of the human body.

**ova** (i) Plural of ovum; (ii) Cricketing reference to number of balls bowled.

**ovary** (i) Place where ova are produced; (ii) Bag in which cricket balls are stored.

**ovulation** (i) Time when the ovum comes out of the ovary; (ii) What happens when you change bowlers.

**ovum** (i) Singular of ova; egg; (ii) Having only one bowl.

**owchyaschlong** Where semen comes from.

**oxytocin** A hormone which encourages uterine contraction and milk production.

**pain** The feeling you get when you stop a high-velocity wet leather soccer ball with your groin. There is a lot of this involved in childbirth. (Pain that is, not soccer balls.)

**paediatrician** A specialist children's doctor who drives an expensive car.

**pelvic floor** The muscles in the base of the pelvis which hold everything together. They are attached to the pelvic walls, pelvic ceiling and pelvic viewing gallery.

**pelvic thrust** Put your hands on your hips and hold your knees in tight. Yep, it almost drives you insa-yay-yay-yay-yay-yane!

**pelvis** The bones of the hips, as shaken widely by Elvis Presley.

**perineum** External skin all around the vagina.

**pethidine** Anaesthetic which is injected.

**phantom pregnancy** When The Ghost Who Walks is about to have children.

**piggin** A wooden pail with a long stave as a handle.

**placenta** The interface between mother and foetus which controls life-support and waste disposal.

**Porsche** The car driven by your paediatrician.

**postnatal** Time after the birth.

**postnatal depression** Depression during the time after the birth.

**post partum** An express delivery service offered by Australia Post.

**praetertranssubstantiationalistically** The act of surpassing the act of transubstantiation.

**pregnant** When a woman has a baby inside her.

**premature** When a baby is born before it reaches adolescence.

**progesterone** A hormone produced in large quantities during pregnancy.

**prostaglandin** A hormone which encourages labour contractions. It is found in prostaglandin gel, pessaries and semen.

**punt** The indentation in the bottom of wine and champagne bottles.

**quadruplets** Four children born from the one pregnancy. This will guarantee you an appearance on a current affairs show.

**quintuplets** Five children born from the one pregnancy. Guaranteed front cover and pictorial in at least two women's magazines.

**Qaqa kwaze laziqukokeqika** Xhosian tongue-twister which translates as: 'The desert rat falls and bursts its larynx'.

**rash** (i) Skin irritation caused by a wet nappy; (ii) Your behaviour the night your baby was conceived.

**Red Nose Day** (i) Fund-raising campaign for SIDS awareness; (ii) What you have the day after the birth if you celebrate too much the night before.

**reverse peristalsis** What you do when you change a nappy that looks like a special effect from a horror film.

**rooting reflex** (i) When pigs poke around in the dirt looking for truffles; (ii) When a baby pokes around on the breast looking for the nipple; (iii) Oh, forget it! You're pathetic.

**SAAB** The car driven by your anaesthetist.

**scrotum** Ugly wrinkly dangly male thing containing the all-important testicles.

**semen** The goopy stuff, containing sperm, that comes out of your penis.

**sex** Memories ...

**show** A sign of the onset of labour. It is when all this blood and mucus and stuff comes out of the woman's vagina. (Think about this the next time someone invites you out to 'see a show ...')

**SIDS** Sudden Infant Death Syndrome.

**sit on a potato pan Otis** A really hilarious palindrome.

**SK-70** The name of a rock band I played in during the late seventies. We reached new heights in anonymity and the crowds flocked to our gigs in their severals.

**sleep-in** I've forgotten what this is. Sorry.

**snappy** Three-pronged clip used to secure a nappy.

**sperm** The male reproductive tadpole. There are about 300 million sperm per human ejaculation, which though impressive is not as awesome as that of the pig, which produces about 45 billion a go. That's billion, not million. The hamster, on the other hand, only has a fairly uninspiring 3000, which is why there are so few hamsters around.

**stirrups** Once used widely by women to get their legs up during birth. Also used by Australian stockmen to get their legs up on a horse.

**stitches** When you get sewn up; usually applicable to the perineum.

**Syntocinin** A synthetic hormone which helps contract the uterus.

**tang** The projecting prong on a tool.

**term** The period of the pregnancy. To go *full-term* is to carry the baby to the end of the pregnancy.

**testicles** You should have two of these unless you played soccer when you were a kid, in which case one is probably wedged back up where it's not supposed to be. This is the storage tank for your sperm; also referred to as the *family jewels, goolies* or *squids*.

**tofu** The most disgusting foodstuff ever invented.

**transition** The painful period between the first and second stages of labour.

**trifecta** Something to do with horse racing and the number three.

**trimester** A third of the full-term of pregnancy; i.e. three months.

**triplets** When you have three kids from the same pregnancy.

**twins** When you have two kids from the same pregnancy.

**ultrasound** The technological wonder that creates a picture of the foetus by using high frequency sound waves. It's like a sonar but instead of looking for enemy submarines, you're looking for hands, feet and a head.

**umbilical cord** The supply line between the mother and the foetus.

**upyabum** The place where enemas and suppositories are put.

**uterus** Thingy where the baby grows; another word for womb.

**vacuum** Used sometimes to suck out wedged babies.

**vagina** Where the penis goes in and the sperm comes out and then nine months later the baby arrives.

**ventouse** Baby removing device.

**vernix** The creamy goop used by newborn babies and cross-Channel swimmers to keep them warm.

**virgin** Your pregnant wife isn't one.

**virgule** The oblique stroke used between words or tractions.

**Volvo** A car driven badly by people who wear bowling hats.

**waters** Euphemism for the fluid inside the amniotic sac. When the waters 'break', all the fluid spills out onto the floor or the expensive lounge suite or wherever the woman happens to be at the time.

**wet nurse** You thought I was going to say 'a nurse who has fallen in the water', didn't you? Well, you're wrong.

**wind** Babies have lots of this. It means they have air in their stomachs and it has to come out via the holes at both ends of their body.

**womb** (i) Another word for uterus; (ii) The airy sound produced when a boomerang whistles past your ears; i.e. *vsoomb, vsoomb, woomb.*

**X chromosome** A genetic sex indicator. All ova are X. If an X sperm fertilises the ovum, the baby will be a girl.

**xylophone** A musical instrument often found on children's alphabet friezes because it is easier to illustrate than xenon, xenophobia or xerography.

**Y chromosome** A genetic sex indicator. If a Y sperm fertilises the ovum, the baby will be a boy.

**You bastard** Term of affection directed at husbands by wives in the throes of labour.

**zarf** A holder for a coffee cup without a handle.

**zebra** A stripey, horse-like animal from the African plains.

**dyslexia** Problem with reading ability, usually associated with letter confusion.

# PARENT EDUCATION FILMS

Your local DVD store is a veritable gold-mine of educational films that can teach you all you need to know about conception, pregnancy, labour and life at home with a new baby. Here are a few suggestions of some to see ... and some not to.

*The Abyss*
When you want a change of pace, this film has NO babies in it.

*Alien*
Watch, and be grateful that human babies aren't born like this.

*Alien Resurrection*
The alien has a baby. Yuk.

*Aliens*
Nothing to do with fatherhood, but is a really great film anyway.

*Alien Seed*
Women are impregnated by aliens. Yuck.

*Babies*
American slop. Young couples struggle through pregnancy, sperm testing, infertility, ultrasounds etc and all is wholesome at the end.

Fairly realistic labour sequence as mother gives birth to a clean eight-month-old!

*Baby*
With a name like this, you'd expect some decent parental education. But no! It's about a dinosaur.

*Baby Boom*
No, not a film about a dynamite truck crashing into a maternity ward. Instead, Diane Keaton is a successful business woman and a competent fulltime mother. Then I woke up.

*Baby of the Bride*
Saccharine drivel of the worst kind as hordes of American soapie stars tip-toe through the land of pregnancy. Do you really want to see a film starring a pregnant Rue McClanahan? In true American fashion, they even made a sequel. (See *Mother of the Bride*.)

*Baby Talk*
Yuppie couple strive for pregnancy. Clichés everywhere. See the special effects wizardry as mother gives birth to a baby with a navel!

*Betsy's Wedding*
This is what lies ahead of you! (See *Father of the Bride*.)

*The Brady Bunch Christmas Special*
Contains the most unrealistic labour sequence ever filmed.

*Breeders*
Close encounters of the pregnancy kind. Pass me that bucket.

*Cactus Jack*
Nothing to do with babies, but it's one of Arnold Schwarzenegger's first films in which he plays a cowboy. Good for a laugh.

*The Colour Purple*
Contains a fairly realistic birth sequence. See Oprah as a young actor.

*Dances With Wolves; The Director's Cut*
A very long film, good for those long nights with a screamer.

*Dolls*
I knew it! The dolls come to life, with horrific consequences!

*Don't Tell Mom the Babysitter's Dead*
Not to be watched before your first babysitting experience.

*Embryo*
Horror flick about an embryo that ... oh, never mind.

*E.T.*
The star looks kind of like a newborn baby.

*Everything You Wanted to Know About Sex, but Were Afraid to Ask*
See Woody Allen play a sperm about to meet his fate.

*The Exorcist*
This is a good film to prepare you for labour.

*From Here to Paternity*
One of the great classics of parental education.

*Father of the Bride*
This is what lies ahead of you! (See *Betsy's Wedding*)

*For Keeps*
Real footage of conception over the credits. Molly Ringwald and her husband try to balance nappies, postnatal depression, work and parenting while their lives fall apart. The birth sequence is quite realistic and even has a real newborn playing the part of the real newborn. Ignore the sequence where Mum holds the baby in her lap in the car.

*Frozen Assets*
Comedy about a sperm bank. Say no more.

*Ginger Ale Afternoon*
Tense fighting between jealous, arrogant chauvinist pig husband and his pregnant wife. The star is the pregnant actress Dana Anderson who spends almost the entire film in a bikini. Has to be seen to be believed!

*The Hand that Rocks the Cradle*
Another not-to-be-watched-before-your-first-babysitting-experience film.

*The Hunt for Red October*
Wonderful underwater epic. The submarines make noises just like inside the womb.

*Look Who's Talking*
Great special effects sequence over the credits of sperm hunting for the ovum followed by the development of the foetus.

*Look Who's Talking Too*
I haven't seen this one.

*Look Who's Talking Now*
I haven't seen this one, either.

*Look Who's Talking 4*
I don't think they've made it yet. I hope they don't. I won't see it.

*Made in America*
Worth seeing just for the great sperm donation sequence. After that, switch it off.

*Maybe Baby*
He's 57, she's 37 and pregnant. Clichés galore!

*Maybe Baby*
Very British comedy from Ben Elton. Joely Richardson struggles to get pregnant.

*Modern Love*
Burt Reynolds AND Rue McClanahan are in this film. Need I say more?

*Mother of the Bride*
Rue is back! The people who made this must have been hard up for cash. Either that or they lost a bet. (See *Baby of the Bride*.)

*Mr Mom*
Michael Keaton plays a full-time dad and finds that it is not as easy as it looks.

*Nine Months*
Hugh Grant is in it. Say no more. Julianne Moore co-stars.

*Parenthood*
Steve Martin shows you what lies ahead for us dads. Great stuff.

*Parents*
Horror guff about bad parental role models who always have lots of leftovers in the fridge.

*Paternity*
Burt Reynolds hunts for an incubator. (See *Modern Love*.)

*Problem Child*
The worst film I've ever seen.

*Problem Child 2*
Even worse than the first one.

*Robin Williams Live*
Includes some comical insights into labour and parenting.

*Rosemary's Baby*
Woman gives birth to the anti-Christ. Don't let your wife see it.

*She's Having a Baby*
One of the best fatherhood education films ever made. Naive father type II faces the trials of sperm testing, birth classes and the hospital experience. Realistic labour sequence and excellent suggestions for baby names over the final credits.

*Spawn*
Woman gives birth to hideous alien. Don't let your wife see this one, either.

*Star Wars: Revenge of the Sith*
Labour sequence of Luke and Leia being born. Then mother dies. Curse that Darth Vader!

*Terminator*
A film about the conception of John Connor.

*Terminator 2*
See how much pregnancy changed Sarah Connor's life.

*Terminator 3*
Just think, he's the Governor of California.

*That's My Baby*
He wants a baby, she wants a career. Avoid.

*Three Men and a Baby*
The best fatherhood education film ever made. Three successful corporate guys (Danson, Guttenburg and Selleck) are thrown headlong into fatherhood. Great insights into feeding, nappies, bathing, shopping, etc.

*Trois Hommes et un Couffin*
The original *Three Men and a Baby*, but in French.

# WHAT MY MATES HAD TO SAY

Since the whole focus of this book is 'the common man's experience' of fatherhood, I thought I would invite all my fathering comrades to have their say as well. I asked them to free-associate about pregnancy, birth, life and whatever else came to mind.

This will also ensure that they buy their own copy of the book, instead of borrowing mine.

So, here it is – the wisdom of those who have walked the road ahead of you. Read it with a grain of salt.

## ADRIAN
*father of Lyndall, six weeks*
From the age of fifteen, I planned out my life ... what sort of job I would like, the type of girl I wanted to marry, and the place where I wanted to live. I fulfilled my plans but then found myself uncomfortably out of control of my life. I feared not being able to plan anymore.

The first part of the pregnancy was really rough, with a threatened miscarriage. I was quite anxious about being at the birth, but I was trusting in someone greater than me. I was praying everything would be OK.

When the day came, Annie's waters broke at home so we scrambled to the hospital. It was really exciting. When we arrived, she was two centimetres dilated. I put on my cossie and got in the shower with her. Then things got wild. It all happened so fast, I was in shock. The pains came hard and sharp. I didn't know what was going on.

Thirty minutes later Lyndall was born. I was overwhelmed. Two hours later I was still gaa-gaa. I was totally occupied with my new family. That was when the doctor pointed out that I was still in my cossie and I should probably put some clothes on.

## AL

*father of Amy, nine, Beth, seven, Gareth, five, and Josephine, two*
My advice? Be around and make it fun to be a kid.

## ANDREW

*father of Zoe, eight weeks*
I was really annoyed that everyone was so negative about how being a dad was going to really change things. I haven't found it to be like that at all. I expected my life to be over. Some things of course have changed, but it's nothing you can't adjust to.

We've just come back from four weeks' hiking and camping, with Zoe bobbing around in a front sling. She survived 4-wheel-driving and a jog down Koszciusko to escape a storm. Our tent even collapsed one night and she didn't even wake up. On one part of the trip, Gaia kayaked while I drove the car with the baby in it down a riverside road. When she needed a feed, I'd just pull over and honk the horn.

I think it's all a matter of attitude. If you focus on the negative and talk yourself into a corner, you'll of course end up being defeatist and looking for problems in the whole thing.

In terms of the birth itself, that was pretty wild. I came home from work and Gaia had walked a few kilometres up to the hospital. I got up there about four in the afternoon and we went through till seven the next morning. We were even sleeping in three-minute bursts between contractions – we were so exhausted.

When Zoe was born, I was just blown away. It was the most awesome thing to see. I've done lots of stuff in my life [at] the four ends of the globe, but the birth was the most amazing thing I've ever encountered.

(*Oh yeah? Let's see if you're still as cocky in six months' time, Mr Smarty Pants PD.*)

## BILL
*father of Talitha, three days*

Everyone keeps telling me that BC stands for 'Before Children'. It makes me nervous and curious as to the changes in our lifestyle. I am hoping and praying that I can meet the challenges and be a good father.

The birth was pretty moving. We went to the hospital and then got sent home again because nothing was happening. By the time we got home, the contractions had started again. We went back to the hospital. That was at 4 pm. Talitha was born around four the next morning. I was surprised that I was invited to 'catch' her on the way out. She was so slimy! I'm glad it wasn't me giving birth.

## DANIEL
*father of Zachary, four months*

Well, I'm not too sure. I think it's some sort of infection. Like a skin disease, with lots of scabs caused by parasites or something ... What? Oh, babies!! I thought you said scabies!!!

## DAVID
*father of Simon, three, and Timothy, fifteen months*

As a father, you don't have to be one of *The Magnificent Seven* ... but here's the good, the bad and the ugly of being a father.

The Good: that magic moment when the head first crowns, the first smiles, first steps, first words and cuddles.

The Bad: sleep deprivation, sleep deprivation and sleep deprivation.

The Ugly: ties stained with breast milk vomit, first solids, leaking nappies.

## ERIC
*father of twins Harrison and Jordan, eight months*

I don't think you can imagine how hard it'll be. I've got seven nieces and nephews, some of whom I helped raise. But holding down a job and living with them 24 hours a day under the one roof ... that's another story.

It's fifty times harder and a hundred times better than I ever imagined.

My advice? Get all the help you can.

## GABI
*father of Daniel, ten, and Joel, seven*

My first thought when I got into the labour room was, 'There's no way that baby is gonna fit through there!' I sure am glad I'm not a woman.

The labour was pretty exhausting. What I remember most is the hunger I felt. Deb went into labour at midnight and twenty hours later I still hadn't eaten. We got all psyched up for a natural childbirth and then they realised the baby was posterior and [had] got into distress, so Deb had to go off for a caesarean. That was a bit unexpected. And to be honest, [there] came a fear that something might go wrong.

When we brought the baby home, it didn't change our lives much. We still made it to restaurants and just put him under the table! The big change was that I used to be a surfer. Gone were the days of getting my board and heading out for an afternoon of waves. Taking a baby to the beach meant umbrellas and bassinettes, clothes … oh, you name it. The surfing had to go.

## GRANT
*father of Alex, three, and William, three days*
Becoming a father is full of unexpected joys and spontaneous pleasures. Children make life simpler but richer. They [bring] less peace but greater fulfilment.

Accept all the advice you can handle, ask for help when you need it, and don't overlook your wife.

## JAMES
*father of Anna, six hours*
The pre-natal classes turned out to be a waste of time because we didn't do any of the stuff we'd practised. She [Sarah] didn't want to be walked or rocked or massaged.

It was frustrating when all the staff were saying, 'Look there's the head' and stuff like that. I couldn't see a thing because Sarah had me in a head-lock. I felt like I was in a rugby scrum.

I was really surprised when Anna was born. She was covered in thick white goop, like glue. She looked like Des Renford getting out of the Channel.

Anyway, it was bloody exciting. Unbelievably emotional. I wouldn't have missed it for anything.

## JAMIE
*superfather of twins Caleb and Daniel, two, and twins Sam and Hannah, eight months*
When Annie started showing at five weeks, everyone started getting suspicious. She grew rapidly. When she had the ultrasound, it confirmed that we were having twins. We were really excited. My only fear was that there were more than two in there. I kept thinking, 'There's one hiding, there's one hiding.' But there wasn't.

But the second time was different. I never, never thought for one moment that we would have twins again ... I thought that it was statistically unlikely and I kept telling myself not to worry.

When I found out, I was in a state of shock. I was numb ... like a zombie. Four kids in two and a half years ... I didn't know anybody who had lived through it. The next morning though, I was fine.

It's such a fantastic moment when your child is born. You hold him up and look into his face for a moment and it's almost like you're holding a mirror. It's such a buzz when the nurses exclaim, 'Doesn't he look like his dad!' To see yourself recreated like this is breathtaking, and it's something that makes being a dad so special.

For me, seeing myself in my kids and sharing so many experiences together, watching them grow and [having] the privilege of looking after them, is what makes being a dad important.

Having four kids in the house ... it's hard, but it's not overwhelming. Our babies have been really good, and it's pretty special holding a baby or two in each arm. It makes you feel ... tall.

## JEFFREY
*father of Nathaniel, four, Tyler, two, and The Bump, minus seven months and counting, foster father of Dugald, 34, and Tyrone W Dawg, four*

They say that nothing can prepare you for being a father. Well, babies don't come with a set of instructions like my software, but I actually think that everything in life prepares you for being a father.

Like, for example, gridiron. You have your first child and it's two on one. That's pretty easy. You have your second and it's one on one. That's still manageable. After that, you get into zone defence plays. The kids know all the moves. Each parent marks one child each, but that still leaves one to wreak havoc. They work it all out beforehand.

Or science. Each kid is like a charged nuclear particle. Their behaviour is dependent on how much space they have to move in, the ambient temperature, how fast they're travelling, how many collisions they have and how many other particles there are in the immediate vicinity. Then you introduce control rods the parents. They absorb all the energy and prevent huge amounts of destruction occurring.

Having a new baby in the house does change things. You miss the little spur-of-the-moment things, even like getting on your bikes and going for a ride. It's physically tiring, but not really exhausting. I mean, it's not too different to studying to get through uni or staying out a lot. But it takes a truck-load of mental energy. Babies demand your attention all the time. You can't just leave them to amuse themselves.

(My favourite age is four to seven months, which is when they're at what I call the Self-Entertaining-Non-Mobile stage. You can put a rattle in their hand and get to the fridge or bathroom for five minutes and you know they'll be where you left them when you get back.)

Being a dad is rewarding and humbling. It's helped me appreciate my own parents and put it all into perspective. You take your own parents for granted, but when you have kids, you realise how much time and effort it takes.

It's an incredible responsibility moulding a person. Scary, but exciting.

## JIM
*father of Michelle, three, and Madeleine, seven months*
Everyone has always heard stories about new fathers and how nothing can really prepare you for it. It makes you appreciate your own parents as you never thought you would. It makes you realise your own selfishness and it gives you a new sense of responsibility.

The birth itself is extremely stressful, mainly because you feel helpless. At the same time, the imminence of the birth itself is really exciting.

I remember a great relief when our baby was born. The pain for my wife was over and our baby had all the right bits and pieces. It is not an experience a woman should go through alone. My baby looked lovely ... not like those ordinary ones that other people have. I mean that. If she was horrible, I'd admit it.

Nowadays, my life has totally changed. No longer do I have all the time to self-indulge the way I used to. There's no doubt I sometimes wish I could get more done, but the time with your kids is worth too much.

*moulding a person – scary, but exciting ...*

## JOHN
*father of Angus, nineteen months*

A 'hood' is a garment. Why then this word is incorporated into the term 'fatherhood' is inexplicable to me. There are no similarities between the state in which I find myself and any garment I have ever worn. Clothing is easily donned and is easily removed at the whim of the wearer. Not so with fatherhood. It is not something into which one slips casually. Once acquired, it is something so integral to one's being that it can never be removed.

Whereas clothing is usually made to fit the wearer, one cannot alter the role of fatherhood to fit oneself. It comes as it comes and one has to adjust to it. It affects every aspect of one's life: daily routines, sleeping habits, social life, finances – nothing escapes the influence of that bundle of joy.

It is something that can never be fully anticipated. All the information and advice in the world (no doubt all contained in Downey's weighty tome!) cannot prepare one for the extremes of emotion at the birth, the mind-numbing exhaustion as one sets off for work after a week of sleepless nights spent having one's ears assaulted by the screams of a baby for whom one doesn't know what to do, and the myriad other experiences that await one on the other side.

So what does fatherhood have to recommend it?

Nothing can prepare you for what is in store when that little face lights up with a smile. The pleasure of fatherhood is so deep and so lasting that it easily surpasses the short-lived pleasure experienced during the baby's creation.

## JOHN
*father of David, five months*

I always thought that when the time came, I would be Superdad and that it would all come naturally to me. It didn't take me long to realise that fathering takes a whole lot of work, frustration, self-sacrifice and humility. It's turned my life upside-down, but I wouldn't give it up for anything.

I've done lots of things in my life which have given me satisfaction and a buzz. Being a dad, however, has been better. It's given me a sense of completeness as a person.

## MALCOLM
*father of Rebecca, two, and Joshua, seven months*

Let me warn you. To go anywhere with kids involves a car-load of strollers, cots, highchairs, changes of cool clothes, changes of warm clothes, sunhats, toys and books. You're going to need a bigger car.

Suddenly your house doesn't seem so big or so clean.

To go anywhere without your kids involves cajoling, persuading and begging friends, family or babysitters. You find yourself staying home a lot.

And I didn't used to consider 6.30 am a sleep-in, either.

But nothing prepared me for my daughter's declaration of, 'I love you Daddy', or the beaming grin that erupts over the face of my son when I walk through the door at night.

## MARK
*father of Laura, three, and Katie, 21 months*
*(Mark is actually overseas at the moment, but I know he wouldn't want to be left out so I wrote something for him in his own biting and largely sarcastic tone of voice – PD.)*

Fatherhood ... ah, who wouldn't want to be a father? It's wrecked my life but who's counting? It's great. Wonderful stuff. No, really. I have the best kids in the world. I enjoy being their dad.

I love the smell of nappies in the morning.

## MARK
*father of Adam, nine, and Matthew, four*
Was it really this hard for my Dad?

## MATTHEW
*father of Jordan, one week*
Look, I'm not particularly fazed about it all. It's been done a million times before. And if everybody else on the planet can do it, we can too.

I don't want our lives to be dictated by the baby. If we go out to dinner, we'll put the baby in its capsule and take it with us. Maybe I'm naive. I don't know. I mean, I know we'll spend more time at home, but I don't want to get locked away like in a fortress or something.

We've been stashing money so Tracey can take time off work, and then I'll take my leave and we'll swap the care-taking. That'll give me about three months solid at home. What a great opportunity!

## OWEN
*father of Sophie, two, and Rosanna, two months*
The worst thing I could imagine about having a baby was not getting enough sleep. So to prepare ourselves for the worst, we fully expected what is referred to in baby-rearing circles as 'a screamer'. I'm not sure if it's possible to store up sleep for a later date, but I calculated [that by the time Sophie arrived] we could [have gone] without a decent sleep-in for about six months.

Strangely, our new arrival had no trouble sleeping through the night sometimes [sleeping] for more than twelve hours straight. We kept tip-toeing into her room to hold a mirror up to her nose to see if she was still breathing. I think we learned that trick off 'Murder She Wrote'.

The moral of the story is: sleep in a lot before the baby comes and don't expect a sleeping angel.

When Rosie came along, I suspected it might not be too much more work. It's more like tag-team parenting now. One stops the other one starts. [The babies] seem to know.

In a way it's twice the work, but it's certainly twice the fun.

## PHIL
*father of Samuel, five, Laura, three, and Cameron, six weeks*
The births have been the most amazing experiences. Just being there has been incredible. We went to a birth centre, where the father plays an important role. I was helping with hot packs, massages, showers, gentle rocking … you know, just being there.

When each of my kids was born, I bawled my eyes out. It's just so miraculous and exciting. You finally see and hold your new baby.

I think it's gotten easier the more kids we've had. The first was a bit of a shock to our domestic sphere but then all the baby stuff crying, nappies, interrupted sleep all became the norm. I've found the third one really easy.

I love being a family man and watching my kids grow up.

## RAY
*father of Lachlan, two*
Parenthood stuffs up your life – *Ray*.

No it doesn't – *Ray's wife*.

Actually, it's parents who stuff up your life – *Ray's son*.

Mind you, I could have done without the competition – *Ray's cat*.

My life is now complete – *Ray's mother-in-law*.

It's the only worthwhile thing he's ever done in his life – *Ray's mother*.

No comment – *Ray's father*.

He should spend more time on his golf swing – *Ray's father-in-law*.

Seriously, before my wife and I stopped using contraception, we asked a few friends what it was like to be parents. The thing they emphasised was that unless you really, really, really, really, really, really want children, you shouldn't have them. This was an understatement.

So if you're about to be a father, there's a hell of a lot of stuff I could tell you to make it easier. But I'm not going to. You can find out yourself. But I'll tell you this:

Every fear you have is worse than you expect, and every hope is better. (*You can't half tell that Ray is a writer – PD.*)

## SANDY
*father of The Unborn, minus six months and counting*
Pascale brought home a home pregnancy kit just to stir me. She'd just come off the Pill so it was a bit of a joke.

The smile was wiped off our faces when the little strip turned purple. We just sat there and stared at it, waiting for it to fade. It didn't.

The next morning she got up and checked it. Still purple. In fact it's been several weeks now, and the damn thing's still purple. We check it every morning. Every morning it's still purple.

It's slowly starting to dawn upon us what this little purple strip means … It's hard to come to terms with. It just … 'happened'. The funny thing is, I don't feel like I'm a 'parent'. I'm just a normal guy.

## SIMON
*just married*
Look Pete, I know I'm not a dad yet but I'm trying really hard, honest! Give us a few years and we'll be right into this parenting thing. Can't I be in your book, please? You put Mal and Sandy in.

## SIMON
*father of Christina, six months*
One of the best things about being a Dad is crashing out in the loungeroom on a Sunday afternoon with my daughter [and] enjoying the rugby together. She is such an enthusiastic spectator; eyes wide, arms flapping and legs kicking. She doesn't care who wins, as long as they wear a red jumper.

Just by being there, my daughter turns an ordinary event into a special one.

What does concern me, however, is how she is in the habit of calling out 'Daddaddadda' to every player on the field.

## WAYNE
*father of Brittainy, eighteen months*
Look Pete, I was going to try to have it ready by tonight but I'm too damned busy being a father. Hey … why don't you just print that?

# INDEX

## A

Afterbirth 127–8
Alcohol, avoiding 40
Amniotic sac 38, 128
Amniotomy 92
Anecdotes
  answering machine in New
    York 2
  author in PD class 8
  author's encounter with a
    busload of American tourists
    111–12
  author getting very very
    frustrated in the middle of
    the night 153–4
  Chicken Marengo 2
  curious aftershave 2
  guy who asks what the silvery
    bucket is for 89
  morning sickness 12
  nappies 160–1
  nesting urge 67
  pain of childbirth 110

Apgar test 129
Aphrodite 187
Appearance of babies 127
Augmentation 92

## B

Babies
  appearance 127
  bathing 76–7, 166–17
  bonding 130–1
  changing 73–4
  clothing 72–3
  crying 146–54
  developmental stages 36–7,
    174–9
  feeding 77–8
  going out with 167–9
  impact on the home and life
    141–3
  playing with 169–71
  weaning 157–8
Baby blues 134–6
Baby proofing the home 179–2

Baby sling or back pack 82–3
Baby walkers 83–4
Beethoven's Fifth 174
Beta hCG 13, 14, 37
Bibs 158
Birth
   celebration following 132
   education classes 89
   expected date of 48
   stages *see* Stages of labour
Birth centres 43
Birth class 88–90, 93
Birth plan 90–1
Birthing positions 90, 93
Blastocyst 37
Bonding 130–1
Bottle-feeding 77, 144–6
Bouncers 78
Brahms's 'Lullaby' 71, 149
Braxton Hicks contractions 115–16
Breast pump 78
Breastfeeding 78, 129, 144–6
Breasts, changes in 54
Breech birth 95
Bucket, nappy 76
Burping 144–6

C
Caesarean delivery 96–7
Cars
   capsule 79–80
   child seat and booster seat
      79–80
   travelling with baby 79–80
Cartoons
   afterbirth planting party 12
   baby as a bad person of history
      100
   Brahms, the sadist 150
   cavemen asking about hot
      water 107
   dad and son having trouble
      bonding 162
   dad celebrating with two
      guitarists 125

   dad feeling his child kick
      39
   dad moulding a person 211
   dad with the "A–Z map of
      woman's insides" 8
   different types of doctor 47
   God being very clever 11
   guy at the *Happy Chook*
      stand 82
   guys wearing *Mega–Teeth*
      t–shirts 73
   pets being jealous 183
   woman in labour 114
   woman in the Labour Ward
      phoning New York 61
   woman sickened by the thought
      of baby waste moving
      through cord 38
*Cat's in the Cradle* 30
Cayapo Indian pain relief method
   110
Celebrating fatherhood 29
Cervix, dilating 120
Change-tables 73–4
Childbirth *see* Labour and
   delivery
Chores 143
Circumcision 102–3
*Clan of the Cave Bear* 106
Cloth nappies 164
Colic 148
Colostrum 129
Communication 22
Conception 8–10, 37
Contractions 115
Cord, cutting 127
Costs 85–6
Cots 71–2
Cradles and cribs 71–2
Crying 146–54

D
*Dads, Toddlers and the Chicken
   Dance* 194
Daughters 34–5

Day bag 80–1
Day care 64–5
Decorations 75
Delivery *see* Labour and delivery
Developmental stages 36–7,
    174–9
Diet 40
Dilation 120
Discrimination on grounds of
    pregnancy 63
Disposable nappies 163–4
Drugs 40
Dual career couples 63

E
Education 86–90, 191
Embryo 37
Endorphin 122, 135
Epidural block 95
Episiotomy 95, 128
Equipment 67–85
Excitement 21, 133

F
Fallopian tubes 9, 35
Family day care 65
Fatherhood 7–199
    advantages and disadvantages
        1–2
    being active and involved 5–6,
        60–2, 150–2
    celebrating 29
    commitment 5
    coping with the labour 121–2
    educating yourself for 86–90,
        191
    emotions on finding out that
        your wife is going to have a
        baby 15–18, 20–3
    involvement 5
    overdoing it at first 132–4
    parenting secret 189–92
    qualifications 30
Fear 21–2
Feeding 77–8

    bottle-feeding 144–6
    breast-feeding 78, 129, 144–6
    burping 145
    solid foods 79, 157–8
Feelers 86
Fertilisation 10, 18
Films, parenting 205–9
Fluffy toys 75–6
Foetus 37–9
Foetal heart monitor 125
Foetal stethoscope 48
Food cravings 27
Forceps 97
Frogs and snails and puppy-dog
        tails 34

G
Games to play with baby 170–1
Genetic information 36–7
Genitals, newborns 127
Greg Brady's den 66
Guests and visitors 45, 137–8
Guilt 21

H
Harold Holt 75
Health cover 43–45
Health during pregnancy 40–2
Health insurance 42–3
Highchair 79
Home births 42–3
Homecoming 138–9
Hospitals
    booking 43–5
    choice of 44–6
    familiarising yourself with 88–9
    feelings about 42
    private 45
    public 44
Humidicrib 98

I
Immunisation 103–4
Implantation 37
Incredible Hulk 154

Income, family 63
Incubator 98
Induction/augmentation 92

J
Jaundice 126
*Jaws*, theme from 17
JFK 75

L
Labour and delivery
  baby removing devices 97
  birthing positions 90, 93
  celebration following birth 132
  definition 42
  don't panic during 117
  history of 106–8
  induction 92
  plan 90–1
  preparing for 89–90
  sex triggering 92
  support during 122–4
Lanugo 127
Lighting 74
*Little House on the Prairie* 117
Lullabies 171–3

M
Maternity leave 63
Meconium 161
Membranes, rupturing 92
Midwives 42
Monitor 74
Morning sickness 12–13, 53
Mortgage repayments 63
Mr Ed, the talking horse 178
Multiple births, chances of 52
Myths 26–9

N
Names for baby 98–102
Nappies 159–66
  buckets 76
  changing 34
  cloth 164

disposable 163–4
nappy service 165
Nesting urge 66–7
Night, baby keeping you up
  during 149–54, 189
Nilsson, Lennart 36
Nursery 70–1

O
Obstetrician
  choosing 46–7
  visits to 47–8
Opossum 57
Ova 9–10

P
Pain 108–10
Pain relief options 93–5
*Parenthood* 29–30, 189
Passive smoking 41
Parenting secret 189–92
Paternal Tunnel Vision 133
Paternity leave 60
Paul McCartney 2, 199
Pets 183–4
Placenta 39, 128
Playpen 84
Photography of the birth 112–15
Postnatal depression 136
Pregnancy
  average weight gain during 54
  breaking news of 23–6
  confirming 13–15
  decisions during 42–9
  drugs and alcohol during 40
  due date 48, 59
  health during 40–2
  hormonal changes 52
  leaving work 63
  length of average 48
  physical and emotional changes
    experienced 52–5
  responses to news of 15–18,
    20, 21–2
  sex during 55–6

test 14–15
trying for 15
Prams 81–2
Premature babies 48
Private patients 44, 45
*Psycho*, theme from 17
Public patients 44

R
Relationship with your wife
    185–6
Rusks 158

S
Scott, Sir Walter 86
Sex
    birth, after 186–8
    pregnancy, during 55–6
    labour, triggering 92
    leading to pregnancy 8–10
    miracle of 10
Sex of child
    determination of 36
    learning 33
Shows 115
SIDS 41, 71–2, 76, 155–6
Sleep
    lack of 149–54, 189
    pregnancy, during 54–5
Smoking, effects 41, 156
Solid foods 79, 157–8
Sons 34–5
Sperm 8–10
Stages of labour
    Stage 1: before the birth
        118–24
    Stage 2: the birth 124–6
    Stage 3: after the birth 126–30
Strollers 81–2

Sudden Infant Death Syndrome
    (SIDS) 41, 71–2, 76, 155–16
Sugar and spice and all things
    nice 34
'Superfather' 27
Synotocin drip 92, 121

T
*Tardis, The* 80
Teething 156, 158
Time management 59–62
Toddlers 194
Toxoplasmosis 30, 40

U
Ultrasound 33–34, 49–52
Umbilical cord 39, 127
Uterus 36–7

V
Ventouse 97
Vernix 126
Videotaping birth 112–15
Visitors 45, 137–8
Visualisation 93–4

W
Waters breaking 115
Weaning 157
Womb 36
World records
    caesarean delivery 96
number of children to one mother
    52
Work
    changes in arrangements 62–6
    post-birth 63
Workaholics 4